Articles Of Encouragement
30 Days of Empowering YOU!

LaTrice Williams

DEDICATED TO ALL PEOPLE

There is a word that God has for every person's life!

AUTHOR'S CONTACT INFO

Email:
LaTriceSpeaks@latricewilliams.com

Main Website:
www.latricewilliams.com

Facebook:
www.facebook.com/LaTriceWilliamsMinistries

Twitter:
https://www.twitter.com/LaTriceSpeaks

ACKNOWLEDGMENTS & SPECIAL THANKS:

To My Lord and Savior, Jesus Christ – Your life saved my life. For loving me through my good and my bad: Thank You. All of my life, I'll serve You. Thank You for not erasing my future because of my past. I give You my highest praise – Hallelujah! Words can't fully express my gratitude and love for my heavenly Father for all of His great blessings and favor upon my life. I could not do what I'm called to without Your Hand guiding me. Thank you, Lord! You always make it happen for me.

To those who served **as Beta Readers**, giving me valuable feedback and input, THANK YOU!

Thank you, **Business Savvy, Inc.**, for this outstanding cover design. I'm grateful for your service in excellence!

To the **LWM Vision Team**, much love and appreciation to you and all that you do to ensure that the visions come to pass! There is greater and more to come!

DAY 1
HOW BAD DO YOU WANT IT?

Reference: 2nd Kings 5:1 & 9-13 NIV

1 Now Naaman was commander of the army of the king of Aram. He was a great man in the sight of his master and highly regarded, because through him the LORD had given victory to Aram. He was a valiant soldier, but he had leprosy.

9-13 ⁹ So Naaman went with his horses and chariots and stopped at the door of Elisha's house. ¹⁰ Elisha sent a messenger to say to him, "Go, wash yourself seven times in the Jordan, and your flesh will be restored and you will be cleansed." ¹¹ But Naaman went away angry and said, "I thought that he would surely come out to me and stand and call on the name of the LORD his God, wave his hand over the spot and cure me of my leprosy. ¹² Are not Abana and Pharpar, the rivers of Damascus, better than all the waters of Israel? Couldn't I wash in them and be cleansed?" So he turned and went off in a rage. ¹³ Naaman's servants went to him and said, "My father, if the prophet had told you to do some great thing, would you not have done it? How much more, then, when he tells you, 'Wash and be cleansed'!"

Is there something in your life that you've been seeking God for, praying for or just longing to achieve? Have you considered if you really want it and what you're willing to do to get it? Have you ever had an issue that you really needed solved but for some reason you could not find an answer? Consider the story found in our scripture reference.

The focus of our reference is Naaman, commander of the army of the King of Aram. He was a hero so to speak. Naaman was depicted as a man of great stature and he was used to getting respect. He was certainly not from the John Legend era that would have said we're just ordinary people.

Naaman was a highly regarded individual who was referred to as honorable; a mighty man of valor. But in all that, Naaman was a man that had an issue but no resolution. He was a leper.

Interestingly enough, Naaman was much like some people today. You have some great characteristics and attributes and you've gotten many accolades as to how well we've done in this area or that one. Some of you may even be well-known, respected popular and sought after but like Naaman, you've got an issue with no resolution.

In this story, Naaman is pointed in the direction of help. The young maiden to his wife said, "if only he would go see the prophet in Samaria, he would cure him of the leprosy," or as I refer to it- his issue.

The bible goes on to says that Naaman went to the King of Aram whom he served and told him what the girl said. The King of Aram sent him to the King of Israel with a letter essentially saying - "cure him". The King of Israel went off. He accused him of picking a quarrel with him saying, "I'm not God. Why is he sending you to me?"

In the midst of all that, Elisha sent word to the King of Israel asking "why are you doing all that? Send him to me and he will know there is a prophet in Israel."

The King of Israel sent Naaman to Elisha- the prophet in Samaria. Keep in mind that this is the same prophet the young maiden advised him to see in the first place.

The Lord said that the answer to your issue is still in the place that He has already told you about. You must learn to follow God's instructions first.

If we examine the reference portion of our scripture for this article, Naaman is standing at Elisha's door. He is essentially standing at the door of his blessing.

My question to you is - are you standing at the door of your blessing? You may be standing at the door of your blessing with your hand on the door knob but you must remember every entrance to somewhere is an exit from somewhere else.

You are going to have to give up something this time to get something else. Either you're going to be bound or free but you cannot be both. You can't go forward while looking backwards.

Consider this analogy- In between drive and reverse is neutral and in neutral, you are not going anywhere. The most that you can do in neutral is coast to a slow stop or have someone to push you around. You'll never be moving forward *fast* to your destiny.

So in our text, Naaman is in neutral - standing at the door of Elisha's house. The Lord wants to know, which way are you going? Are you even moving at all? Have you neutralized yourself with limited thinking? Maybe it's because the blessing has not come in the manner in which you desired?

As you look at Naaman's story and his reaction while standing at the door of his blessing - I wonder, will you see yourself?

While you are standing at the door, waiting like Naaman for something great or grand to happen, the Lord said consider this- He may not come the way you want Him to.

If you remember in Naaman's story, a messenger came to the door instructing him to go and wash in the Jordan River seven times and he would be clean.

Whoa? What the world? Can you imagine the look of shock and horror on Naaman's face?

Immediately Naaman got mad! It's similar to how you tend to react when somebody says something you don't like or don't agree with. You go straight into "I know he didn't say what I think he said," complete with eye popping, neck rolling and sometimes some pouting.

The Lord said it's time to change how you respond to His instructions whether you like them or not; whether you like how they came to you or who they came through or why you think they said it to you. How you respond to God in your attitude and your actions will determine the results that you will get.

Can you imagine Naaman going into a rage? Not only was he told to go wash in the Jordan but Elisha sent a messenger! The Lord said that some of you are just as self-righteous, self-absorbed, and arrogant as Naaman.

Naaman was appalled! Not only did Elisha tell him to go wash in the Jordan, he sent a messenger! Elisha didn't even bother to come out and greet him. Naaman said, "I thought for sure he thought he'd come out and lay hands on me, call on the name of the Lord but he sent a messenger." A messenger of all things! And then to tell him - Naaman, the commander of the army, a hero, a mighty man of valor to go to the Jordan River. The little, dirty, filthy Jordan River! Surely he must have thought - well I never!

God wants some of you reading this to know that you never will with that attitude.

Let me pose this question to you. Which one of God's messengers have you rejected because you didn't like the message or the way it came to you? Don't you know that just because you didn't agree doesn't mean that it was wrong? The Lord said that some of you will miss your true blessing just because you didn't like God's answer.

And for the person that may be saying, I didn't hear God say it, the Lord said no ma'am and no sir; you just didn't receive it through the person who relayed the message.

Too often we fail to see that what we need is in what God said and not who He said it through.

Too many people respond like Naaman. Why can't I do it this way? This way would be better.

The Lord said who do you think you are? Why do you think you're better than anyone else? What makes you think that the word that He gave you isn't the avenue or answer to your issue? The Lord said get over yourself! Just because you don't like it, the way it looks or the way it feels doesn't mean it's not His answer.

The Lord said that He keeps telling you that His thoughts are not your thoughts; His thoughts are higher than yours.

He did not promise that you would like it. He did not promise that it would feel good. He *did* promise that it would all work together for your good. So, how dare you look down on the solutions that God gave you?

While you are wasting time like Naaman did wondering whether he could go wash in another river and still be cleaned, the Lord said you can do it your way if you want to but you will not get His results. If you want God's results, you must follow God's orders. His answer is still the same.

You're going to miss the message looking at the messenger. You're going to miss your blessing, focusing on where it came from. You're about to miss your word from God looking at the person He sent it through rather than hearing the God in them.

How many times have you dismissed God's instructions because it didn't come through the vessel of your choice or from the person you expected it to come from?

I am the messenger sent by God to ask you - **How bad do you want it**?

Naaman needed to be free of his disease but until he decided to do it God's way, he did not get God's results. So how bad did he really want it?

Ask yourself, why are you still sick? Why are you still depressed? Why are you still holding all of that stuff inside of you when God has given you His answer? It's probably the way you responded or perhaps it's your lack of response.

Someone is about to lose their mind but you won't talk to God, Jesus, the elders, the neighbors and anyone else. You are holding in stuff that's about to break you to the core but you're worried about what somebody is going to think or say about you. Yet here you are saying - I can't get any help.

This is not to say that you have to tell everyone you're business but the Lord has given you someone or some people who really care about you despite your distrust of people in general and what you might think of them. Remember that everyone is not the last person you dealt with and everything is not always what it seems.

There are some dreamers reading this right now and at this moment you are wishing and longing to do this and that. You have some great ideas locked up in you. You want to be more active but you just don't want to deal with this person and that person. You don't want to go through all the channels and changes or encounter the obstacles and roadblocks but I ask you again - **How bad do you want it**?

Some of you look at television and say that you would love to do that but you haven't been to one audition, casting call - nothing. You are sitting in church saying I sure would like to sing a song but you haven't gone to one rehearsal.

Will you be like Naaman, resisting the message because it didn't come the way you wanted it? Will you be like him, appalled because it wasn't what you wanted to hear or it wasn't what you planned or expected? Beloved of God - why are you asking God, if you don't really want His answer?

How long have you delayed getting to your answer because you did not follow God's instructions first?

Are you ready to humble yourself today before the Lord? Will you accept that sometimes it cost what it cost to get to God? Are you willing to do what it takes to get all that He has for you?

Will you have the audacity to be like the woman with the issue of blood? Will you step out into a place that you've been told you couldn't be? Remember that she pressed her way to Jesus because she wanted her healing.

Will you, today, be like the two blind men who answered yes Lord when Jesus asked- do you believe I am able to do THIS? It didn't matter what THIS was, the only thing that mattered was that they believed.

Beloved, that's what God wants you to do. Believe! Naaman's story wasn't about how great he was, how well he fought nor was it about the condition he held in his body. It was about the condition of his heart to believe God no matter how He said what He said or whom He said it through.

Remember that according to *your* faith will it be done unto you.

Beloved, ***how bad you want it***? Enough to believe? Enough to follow God's instructions first? Enough to look beyond *how* the message comes as long as you know it came from God?

God said He told you to believe. He told you to let it go and move on, it's killing you anyway. If you change the way you think, it will change the way that you receive.

The Lord is asking you right now - what are you willing to do? How far are you willing to go? How much of **YOU** are you willing to let go of? *How bad do you want to be free of your issue?*

We talk about freedom often but we rarely live *in* freedom. Are you ready to do what God said to be free?

In the end of the story, Naaman went and washed in the dirty, filthy Jordan and the Bible says that he came out clean.

Will make up your mind to do it Gods way? Only you have the answer. *How bad do you really want it?*

I pray that you've been encouraged to reevaluate some answers that you've already received from God. Did you reject them because of the vessel they came through? Did you reject it because it wasn't the answer that you wanted? Keep in mind that just because you didn't like it doesn't mean that it wasn't what you needed.

Prayer: Father, help me to accept the answers that You have already given me. Forgive me for dismissing Your message and Your messenger. Help me to do the things that You've given me to do and to believe that I will get Your results. Lord, help me to give up ME so that I can have more of You and what You desire for my life. In Jesus name, Amen.

DAY 2
YOU ARE NOT ALONE

Reference: John 19:26-27 KJV

[26] When Jesus therefore saw his mother, and the disciple standing by, whom he loved, he saith unto his mother, Woman, behold thy son! [27] Then saith he to the disciple, Behold thy mother! And from that hour that disciple took her unto his own home.

When you think of being alone, it is often associated with loneliness. However if you would closely examine the two, there is a major difference even with the many similarities.

According to Webster's definition, you tend to feel lonely and alone when you are isolated or solitary. You may feel lonely when you are single or seemingly unaccompanied. You feel alone sometimes when you are away from others or by yourself.

Although Webster's definition holds some accuracy and you may experience some of those feelings and emotions of being lonely and alone, the Word of God says that for you, God's children, that's impossible. How is it impossible? Simply because God said that He will never leave you nor forsake you.

You may be experiencing a time in your lives that things or people seem to be breaking away or falling off and because of that you may feel alone. God said it's really not what you think. It's a part of the preparation process for the places that He's about to take you. God just wanted to remind you that, while you're in this transition - *you are not alone*.

The Lord said for everyone that He has called and commissioned to work and greatness, you have this one assurance - He will be with you.

Don't let the appearance of being alone change your mind about what He said - *you are not alone*!

As God was with Moses when He sent him to lead the children of Israel from bondage, He's already with you.

Whether you stand before the nations or the neighborhood, proclaiming His name - God said just as He told Jeremiah, He has put the words in your mouth. He is with you and will rescue you.

To every dreamer, it's time to go ahead and make your dreams a reality. You must stop letting people talk you out of your destiny. Don't allow anyone to speak foolishness into you. So what if they say that you only want to be a star or that you only want to make a name for yourself.

God said get that foolishness out of your ears, your hearts and minds. Remember this - you don't even have the capacity to dream up, think up or imagine what God has planned for you. This is not a matter of you being arrogant; this is a matter of you being obedient.

Be cognizant of this; this is the Lord's work and what He has said is all that should matter and God said greater works shall you do!

When they laugh at you and criticize or put you down for being obedient to the call, remind yourself of two things - it's all a part of getting to the greater and *you're still not alone*.

God said when they do that to you, when they mock your commitment to something other than them, He's just showing you, as He showed Joseph, who is for you and who really isn't.

When your so called family hates you or hates *on* you because of your dream and your parents, whether natural or spiritual don't even encourage your dreams or destiny, God said to remember Joseph. He was with Joseph and everything he put his hands to was successful.

God said when you start to feel alone on your way to your promise, remember Joseph. He was locked in prison and for a while, there was a cupbearer and baker and after a while even they were released. One was released to live and one was released to die but Joseph appeared to have been forgotten. It appeared that Joseph was yet again left alone like he was in the pit. God said to remind you, beloved, that He's working on your entrance into the place that He's already shown you.

More importantly, God wants you to remember that He's ALREADY THERE! *You are not alone* now and *you won't be alone* in the place that He's sending you to.

Consider this also, God has already said He's with you and He's also giving you some people to walk this vision out with you. Now here's the bad news - most likely it's not who you think or who you want it to be. But what you should do is consider those who *are* around you.

Do you remember when Jesus was on the cross and in John 19:26-27, He said the words, woman, behold thy son, son behold thy mother?

God wants you to know that He has appointed some people just for you. When you don't quite feel like you can see the evidence of Him, check out who He has placed around you. You have a representative from the Master!

The Lord said NO! *You are not alone*!

This is how you will know that God has appointed or assigned someone to you because you can trust the ones that stayed with you at the cross or during the cross period.

Check the record of who really had your back at all cost. Who was there when you were going through and you seemingly had nothing to offer them? Who stayed with you when it looked like you were all washed up and down for the count? More importantly, who was there when it cost them more to stand with you than it will ever benefit them?

During the times of trouble and affliction, God said check out who is around you! You may be about to throw away the wrong person and you might just miss God if you do!

God said that you have been looking with your natural eye but He made you a promise and He will keep it. He will be with you! Look again through His eyes.

He already had someone praying for you in those times when you were so devastated that you couldn't or wouldn't pray for yourself.

God had already purposed it in somebody's heart to bless you, to cover you and to protect you.

He had already positioned somebody to take care of you and to watch over you.

Be reminded that this is the Lord's word and this is the Lord's glory! He stands on His Word to perform it. Because His word says that He that has begun a good work in you shall complete it 'til the day of Jesus Christ, He can't leave you alone!

God has work to do *in* you and you have work to do *for* Him!

No matter what it looks like, no matter how it hurts right now, no matter what you think you have lost or are lacking, He said, be assured, ***you are not alone***!

Just as Jesus made sure that His mother and beloved disciple were cared for, He will do the same for you.

Put your trust in Him, believe Him without doubting and rest in Him knowing that in every place that He sends you and for every work that He has assigned to your Hands, God is with you. ***You are not alone***.

14

Prayer: Father, In Jesus name, I thank You for reminding me that I am not alone. I receive Your word that You are with me and will never leave me. Thank You for the things that You have assigned to my hands and the places You have planned for me to go. I pray for Holy boldness and a humble spirit as You guide me into what You've planned for me. Thank You for being with me, for leading me and sticking closer to me than any brother or friend. In Jesus Name. Amen.

Day 3
An Inside Job

Reference: Matthew 26:47-54 NIV

⁴⁷ While he was still speaking, Judas, one of the Twelve, arrived. With him was a large crowd armed with swords and clubs, sent from the chief priests and the elders of the people. ⁴⁸ Now the betrayer had arranged a signal with them: "The one I kiss is the man; arrest him." ⁴⁹ Going at once to Jesus, Judas said, "Greetings, Rabbi!" and kissed him. ⁵⁰ Jesus replied "Do what you came for, friend."[d] Then the men stepped forward, seized Jesus and arrested him. ⁵¹ With that, one of Jesus' companions reached for his sword, drew it out and struck the servant of the high priest, cutting off his ear. ⁵² "Put your sword back in its place," Jesus said to him, "for all who draw the sword will die by the sword. ⁵³ Do you think I cannot call on my Father, and he will at once put at my disposal more than twelve legions of angels?⁵⁴ But how then would the Scriptures be fulfilled that say it must happen in this way?"

I'd like to use an illustration from an old favorite movie released in 1996 entitled Set it Off! Many of you may remember it and if you're like me, you still love it even now.

This popular movie was centered on four young women who desired a better life. The problem was that they made some terribly wrong decisions in an effort to obtain it.

You may remember that these four young ladies had gotten to a point that they felt as if they had nothing left. This was because of some of life's events and changes. One of them lost her brother, another one was fired and they all ended up working at a dead end job and they wanted more.

Let me interject that at the point that you feel like you have nothing left, that's a good place to begin. When you get to the end of you, that's where God begins.

In this movie, one of the young ladies was fired from her bank position. But before she was fired, there were some intricate details that she was privy to as an employee. She knew the layout of the bank, the routines of the workers - the inner workings so to speak. She knew who did what, when and where and she also knew the protective mechanisms they had in place and how to get around them.

As a disciple, Judas was privy to the comings and goings of Christ. He knew where to find him and when.

In the movie, the ladies knew when it was a good time to strike, which tellers to address and which security guards would be a problem. Likewise, Judas knew the hour that Jesus would be in the garden and who would be with him.

Both the ladies in the movie and Judas had what appeared to be a strategically planned takeover but I like to refer to it as *an inside job*!

Those robberies could not have been pulled off so well, accurately timed or garnered so much cash if it had not been for the inside information. Likewise, because of Judas, the chief priest thought that they had setup the perfect capture of Jesus.

God said to tell you that He let you experience that betrayal to show you who was for you and who wasn't.

The Lord wants me to share with you that the things that have been happening in your life are all a part of a strategic plan. The things that have happened and will happen are a result of *an inside job*.

The difference between your life and that of those four women is that this plan has not been designed so that you would end up in a hostage situation, a battle for your life or on the run. This *inside job* was allowed to make you free!

Some things in your life could only be manifested from the inside out. Simply said, God had to do a work *in* you so that His word that He spoke *about* you could come to pass.

In the words of Jesus, it had to happen this way!

All of the things that you've seen, all of the trials, the pressures and the challenges that you've encountered had to happen *this* way to change you on the inside.

None of what you lost had anything to do with what you lost. The houses, the cars, the jobs, the relationships - none of that was really relevant. God said that you had to pass this way to get to the place that He has called you to.

There were some things that absolutely had to be let go of so that you could move on. *God said this was an inside job to get to YOU!*

God said that He could have rescued you a long time ago. He could have put an end to all of this but how would you have become who He chose you to be? How would you have become holy? How would you have become righteous? How could He have purified you if He didn't take you through the fire?

Beloved, this was indeed an inside job and it had to happen this way.

You may have thought that all of this was a trick or a trap of the enemy but God said no! Some of this was allowed so that you would grow into the person that He knew even before He formed you.

God allowed you to experience what felt like abandonment and isolation, not because you were really abandoned or isolated but, because you were set apart!

He said that there is a reason that even though you wanted to remain in the background, without position and title, you kept finding yourself in the front. It was because He had already appointed you.

Yes, the Lord said this was an ***inside job!***

Don't you understand that because He knew you before He formed you; He already knew that His perfect creation would operate in some imperfections in its flesh? The Lord said do not worry because He that has begun a good work in you shall complete it until the day of Jesus Christ.

He said this is why it had to happen this way and it had to be an inside job.

You had to endure sickness so that you would know that He's *the* healer.

You had to endure some lack so that you would know that He's *the* provider.

You had to endure some low self-esteem and hurt feelings so you would know that He's the lifter of your head.

You had to have some battles and warfare so that you'd learn how to put on the whole armor. This fight is not a flesh fight so He had to teach you how to war in the spirit.

It had to happen *THIS* way!

You had to feel like you were losing your mind so that you could put on the mind of Christ. Beloved, when you put on the mind of Christ, it changes the way you *think* which also changes the way you *are* because so a man thinketh - so is he! God said that He had to get you to think like Him so you could *be* like Him!

Your heart had to be broken, so that He could take out that stony heart and give you a heart of flesh.

He had to let you experience bondage so you wouldn't take freedom for granted.

He had to let you feel what felt like the fires of hell so you would accept His gift of eternal life.

He had to let you feel weak so when He strengthened you, you wouldn't forget to reach back.

You had to be in relationship with and maybe even marry the wrong one, so you'd be able to identify the right one.

He had to cause you to seek Him in His word so that you would be thoroughly equipped for every good work!

The bottom line is that your plan had to fail so that Gods plan could succeed.

People of God, this ***inside job***, the inner workings and intricate details of YOU had to happen this way so that what God said about you could be fulfilled and the Glory of God would be revealed in you.

Remember when Jesus said to His disciples - this thing was done for the glory of God.

It had to happen this way. It was just an ***inside job*** to get to you!

Prayer: Eternal God our Father, thank You for working on me. Thank You for not allowing me to stay in the place that I was in or in the shape that I was in. Lord, thank You that although I've been hurt, I'm also healed. Thank You, Lord, for allowing me to see that if I hadn't been through the suffering with You, I wouldn't be able to reign with You. Help me to always remember not only what You've done for me but what You've done in me. Thank You, Jesus, that because of You, I'm a better me. In Jesus Name. Amen.

DAY 4
LET IT GO AND MOVE ON

Reference: Philippians 3:7-14 NIV

7 But whatever were gains to me I now consider loss for the sake of Christ. 8 What is more, I consider everything a loss because of the surpassing worth of knowing Christ Jesus my Lord, for whose sake I have lost all things. I consider them garbage, hat I may gain Christ 9 and be found in him, not having a righteousness of my on that comes from the law, but that which is through faith in Christ- the righteousness that comes from God on the basis of faith. 10 I want to know Christ – yes, to know the power of his resurrection and participation in his sufferings, becoming like him in his death, 11 and so, somehow, attaining to the resurrection from the dead. 12 Not that I have already obtained all this, or have already arrived at my goal but I press on to take hold of that for which Christ Jesus took hold of me. 13 Brothers and sisters, I do not consider myself yet to have taken hold of it. But one thing I do: Forgetting what is behind me and straining toward what is ahead, 14 I press on toward the goal to win the prize for which God has called me heavenward in Christ Jesus.

Let's look at the dynamics of what Paul was writing and the place from which he was writing from. This particular letter was written during Paul's imprisonment in Rome. What Paul wrote in this letter is important but God said we need to look at the *place* that he was in. He was in jail. Locked up. Bound.

I want to speak to you in your place of bondage today- that place that you're locked up and trapped in. Today, I want to strengthen and encourage you in your faith.

Some people are in bondage and don't even realize it. You're locked up in your mind, in your heart and in your spirit. God said that this is the day that He is declaring you free.

Beloved, it's time to **let it go and move on**!

Some of you are locked up in your money and even more of you are locked up in your emotions. You are disgruntled, depressed, broken and discouraged. You've been ready to give up and throw in the towel. You've created your own prison of guilt. Too many of you have locked yourself up in the past and Paul encourages you, even in this state of life, by faith - press on.

I'm sure you may be asking, how do you press? How do you **let it go and move on**?

Paul said, first you must forget those things which are behind you. You've got to get rid of the old stuff, the old way of thinking, the memory of old things done and sometimes the old people in your life.

What's behind you is behind you. Leave it there. The good and the bad. It's time to let go of what you had, what you lost, who you loved and lost, and even what you've done. It's time for you to release the hurt, the pain and the memories. God said it's behind you - leave it there.

If what's behind you didn't make it into your present, then it can't fuel your future.

Let it go and move on!

You may be the one who is stuck on what you used to have. It could be the money that you used to make or the position that you used to hold. You are living so far in what would have, should have and could have that you're blinded to what is to come and you're missing out on your right now.

Not only are today's promises of God passing you by but you have no vision for the future. So that claim that you so boldly made that you are walking by faith and not by sight - God said hold up – there are some things that are hindering that walk.

Today is the day that God is saying *let it go and move on*!

You are letting what has already been, hinder you and keep you from what is to come.
Come out of your past! The good, the bad and the indifferent. It's time to start forgetting.

Beloved, you must free yourself! ***Move on***! Move out! Move away and *let it go*!

Let go of that guilt and shame of the past. Stop letting other people drag you back to where you used to be.

You can't base your move on somebody else. Everybody's move isn't the same. Only you know what you truly need to move out of. Only you know what you need to let go of.

Paul also said forgetting "those things." Beloved, those things are not always negative. There are some good times and some good people in our lives but they may not belong in your *now*. They may not be ordained for your future. What was *good* then may not necessarily be for what's *greater* ahead.

Beloved, you've got to stretch this faith you claim to have and believe what God has said.

23

If you are really walking by faith and not by what you see with your carnal eye, then why are you carrying so much baggage from behind you? Why are you weighted down with things that don't belong to you?

Why are you holding on? Exactly *what* are you holding on to?

Sadly, some of you have even picked up things that belong to other people. You were just "helping" and you ended up carrying it. You're carrying *it* in your thoughts. You wake up thinking about *it*, go to bed thinking about *it* and you can't focus because you're thinking about *it*. You're carrying *it* in your heart, you're consumed with *it*, and you're up and down sometimes because of *it*. An "it" that doesn't even belong to you.

I dare you to get your *"it"* in mind and make a conscious decision to **let it go and move on**!

God said that does not belong to you. That weight is no longer yours. That burden is not yours to carry. Today- put it where it belongs; behind you! **Let it go and move on**!

Here is what Paul says next - Press Forward! Now is not the time to stop. Now is not the time to give up or to throw in the towel. God said don't **you** give up on **you** - not when you're this close.

Beloved, don't you go back to Egypt! God brought you out to bless you. He said get your mind off of what they said and what they did.

Paul said it like this in Philippians 4:8 - think on these things; whatsoever things are good, whatsoever things are honest, of good report, whatsoever is true, pure and right, think on these things!

Beloved, there is a way to **let it go**! There is a way to **move on**! There is a way to walk by faith and not by sight!

Regardless of what you see with your natural eye, your faith should look beyond that and see what God said.

Instead of only seeing that you've got more bills than money, your faith must declare that your God will supply all of your needs according to His riches in Christ Jesus.

Although you feel the pain in your body, your faith must declare that by His stripes you are healed.

It may feel like the attack of the enemy is trying to kill and trying to destroy you but your faith must believe that Jesus came that you might have life and life more abundantly.

God said that there is one more thing for you to do to help you while you're moving on and stretching your faith. It is one word from 1st Thessalonians 5:16 - Rejoice!

In everything give thanks for this is the will of God in Christ Jesus concerning you!

Beloved, *let it go, move on* and rejoice!

While you're leaving the past behind - Rejoice!
While you're shaking off that old mind - Rejoice!
While you're stepping out of your old house - Rejoice!

Every step you take forward- Rejoice!
While you're forgiving that past hurt - Rejoice!
While you're leaving the old behind - Rejoice!

But how do I rejoice, you ask? How do you rejoice while you're dealing with all of that? Beloved, press through and give Him the highest praise. Hallelujah!

Yes, Hallelujah! You must keep this praise on your lips.

It's time to declare that I'm pressing forward! Hallelujah!
You're believing by faith! Hallelujah!
Old things are passing away! Hallelujah!
All things are becoming new! Hallelujah!

You can walk new! You can talk new! You can think new! Hallelujah!

God knows your struggle but keep rejoicing!

When I was growing up in church there was a lady who sang the song - *Don't wait 'til the battle is over - shout now*! Toward the end of the song she would be shouting and singing and then she would say *Hallelujah*!

Then she'd say it again - *Hallelujah*! I remember the words clearly. She'd say, *I thank Him for the rain, I thank Him for the pain, I thank Him for the fire that He brought me through*! She would be rejoicing and often within the song, she'd say *Hallelujah*!

I encourage you to praise Him and rejoice through your trials.

Thank Him for the rain as you're putting it all behind you! Hallelujah! Thank Him for the pain as you're letting it all go! Hallelujah! Thank Him for the fire that He brought you through! ***Move on***! Hallelujah!

It's time to break free! Don't miss this moment, right in the place that you're in - your living room, your bedroom, wherever you are - the presence of the Lord is there and there is liberty available for you!

Don't take this present - this gift, for granted because the past could have, should have and would have taken you out but God has declared you free! Rejoice!

The abuse was supposed to scar you for life but Hallelujah you are healed!

The molestation and rape was supposed to render you useless but Hallelujah you are useful in God's Hands!

The pride was sent to enslave you to yourself but Hallelujah you are free!

The anger was meant to eat you up from the inside out but Hallelujah you are free!

The guilt was meant to silence you but Hallelujah you are free from what had you bound!

The fear was meant to stop you but Hallelujah fear is not a factor any longer!

The lies and ostracizing was supposed to destroy your character but Hallelujah the weapons didn't work!

The failed love and marriage was supposed to close your heart up but Hallelujah God has healed your emotions!

The abandonment was supposed to make you feel alone but Hallelujah He'll never leave you nor forsake you! You are not alone.

Tell yourself that was then and this is NOW!

HALLELUJAH!

Beloved are you truly letting go? Are you going to move on? Are you ready to walk by faith and not by what you see? God said come on out of that place! Forget those things! Reach forward! Live in this hour! Live in this season - in this moment!

What you lost, *who* did it and *how* they did it will no longer weigh you down. Put it behind you! *Let it go*! ***Move on*** and Rejoice! Hallelujah!

Paul said I press toward the mark of the prize of the high calling in Christ Jesus. I encourage you, my friend, to get in your press, ***let it go and move on***!

Prayer: Precious Father, In Jesus name, I pray that the chains of my past will be loosed and the shackles will fall off! I decree in the name of Jesus that I am free! Lord, help me to move on. Help me to let it all go. I will no longer be bound because You, God, have set me free! Lord, I thank you in advance and I'm rejoicing and giving you the highest praise of Hallelujah! In Jesus Name. Amen!

Day 5
Restoration is Coming

Reference: John 11: 38-44

38 Jesus, once more deeply moved, came to the tomb. It was a cave with a stone laid across the entrance. 39 "Take away the stone," He said. "Lord," said Martha, the sister of the dead man, "by this time there is a bad odor, for he has been there four days." 40 Then Jesus said, "Did I not tell you that if you believe, you will see the glory of God?" 41 So they took away the stone. Then Jesus looked up and said, "Father, I thank you that You have heard me. 42 I knew that You always hear me, but I said this for the benefit of the people standing here, that they may believe that you sent Me." 43 When He had said this, Jesus called in a loud voice, "Lazarus, come out!" 44 The dead man came out, his hands and feet wrapped with strips of linen and a cloth around his face. Jesus said to them, "Take off the grave clothes and let him go."

When you think of restoration, it is considered something being given back, being made to look new or put back in its original state.

28

If it's a house, it may be called remodeling or renovation. If it's an addict, it may be called rehabilitation or recovery. If it's something that has been torn down, it's referred to as rebuilding.

The whole point of restoration is to put something back where it belongs or give something back to its rightful owner. It's a return.

God is saying that He's about to put *you* back in your rightful place in the Kingdom. You've been pushed aside, pushed around and even pushed to the back but it's time for you to be in your place. The dead season is just about over. It's almost done.

As soon as this season is up, God said that He's going to do just what He promised. There will be no delay in the manifestations of His promise.

You may not understand it all right now; things may appear to be out of order and falling apart but be assured that God has it all in control. As He said in His word in Jeremiah 29:11, He has it all planned out.

God has plans to take care of you. When you think of taking care of someone or something you may think of providing for them. You may think of giving them a home, food, clothes, shoes, etc. God said that He has already made every provision for you both now and forever more!

Right now, He's about to give you back some things that were taken from you and some things that you willingly gave up.

One of the first things God wants to restore to you is your identity. The Lord said that He wants to remind you of who you are. You are fearfully and wonderfully made. You are a royal priesthood and a holy nation. You are an heir of God and co-heir with Christ Jesus.

Beloved, allow God to restore your confidence to you!

in God's eyes, you are like Abigail - you are wise and beautiful. You are like Hannah - vindicated by the Lord. You're like Deborah - you're an ordained leader. And you are like Esther - you are called for such a time as this. You were built to handle every challenge that is coming your way. You were made to handle the trials, the tribulations, the problems and the issues.

You really are the head and not the tail. You are still above and not beneath.

God said that He's getting ready to give you back everything the cankerworm and the enemy stole from you and everything he thought he killed *in* you.

God is well aware that you don't see any of that. All you see right now is where you are, what's going on in your life, what you need and what you don't have. But the Lord said hold on and be assured - ***restoration is coming to you***!

God knows that you feel like you've been in the dry place but He has not forgotten your faithfulness. He has seen you when you've prayed and praised your way through. He knows the times that you've been weak and wanting to give up. He saw your faith when you kept holding on. You continued to seek Him even when you felt like you couldn't find Him. Beloved, the Lord said He is not slack concerning His promises. ***Restoration is coming***!

There is a scripture in Isaiah 35:2 that says like a crocus it will burst into bloom. When something burst, it has either been building under pressure or it appears to happen immediately.

God said that He has been building you under this pressure. There are some things that are coming after this season that He's going to immediately restore to you.

He's about to call back to life some things that appear to have died in your life. He's about to rejuvenate some of your dreams and passions.

One word of caution: Do *not* try to revive or restore things or people on your own. God said this is His plan. It must be done God's way.

Some things, some people, some relationships, some businesses and some habits need to stay buried but fret not because God knows what you have need of. He knows what you need, when you need it and how you need it. Beloved, He knows.

Some of that stuff had to die so that the things that God wanted in your life could live.

This is about to be a Lazarus experience for you! Just as Jesus specifically called Lazarus out of the grave, there are some specific things God is about to resurrect in your life. There are some specific people He's about to restore back to your life and there are specific parts of *you* that He's calling back to life!

It's time for YOU to come back!

Too often we only view restoration as getting thing back or having people coming back but God said in this time of restoration, He's calling YOU back!

He's calling you to live, calling you to prosper, calling you to be in good health and to have wealth!

This restoration isn't about *what* you get or *who* comes with you - this time of restoring is all about YOU. It's about where you've been, what has happened *IN* you and where God is getting ready to take you!

God said that He had to let you experience this dead season. It was necessary for all of these things to happen. In other words, Lazarus had to die so that you would believe Him and Uzziah had to die so that you would see Him!

Jesus asked Martha, "didn't I tell you that if you believe, you would see the glory of God?" Beloved, He was just trying to get you to see His glory.

There was a need for you to endure. You had to be tried. These tests were necessary. The valley, the desert and the dead season - they were all allowed so that you would believe.

Now is the time that He wants to restore you! God wants to give you back the joy of your salvation, to give you back the freedom of your ability to love without fear and to restore to you the peace of your mind. God wants to give YOU back to YOU!

He has come to erase the stains that have been left on your heart. The YOU that you lost, the YOU that was stolen from you, the YOU that died in the midst of all that was going on, the Lord said Lazarus, it's time for YOU to come forth!

31

He has come to restore you! You, His anointed vessel, His blessed one, His chosen one. It's time for the grave clothes that have been holding you bound to let you go. He's restoring to your freedom to you.

People of God, your restoration is coming!

I only have one question as I close this article - Beloved, Will you be restored?

Prayer: Precious Father, thank You for restoration. I receive everything that You have for me in Jesus name. I thank You that You are beginning a revival in me and that life is being restored to me. Help me to daily receive Your restoration for my life. Help me, Lord, to walk in what You have for me. Thank You for giving me back to me. I'm grateful for Your love and kindness toward me. In Jesus name, I'm taking off my grave clothes and everything that has held me bound. I receive my restoration in Jesus Name. Amen.

Day 6
Ask the Lord to Help You

Reference: Matthew 8:1-13 NIV

When Jesus came down from the mountainside, large crowds followed him. ² A man with leprosy[a] came and knelt before him and said, "Lord, if you are willing, you can make me clean." ³ Jesus reached out his hand and touched the man. "I am willing," he said. "Be clean!" Immediately he was cleansed of his leprosy. ⁴ Then Jesus said to him, "See that you don't tell anyone. But go, show yourself to the priest and offer the gift Moses commanded, as a testimony to them." When Jesus had entered Capernaum, a centurion came to him, asking for help. ⁶ "Lord," he said, "my servant lies at home paralyzed, suffering terribly." ⁷ Jesus said to him, "Shall I come and heal him?" ⁸ The centurion replied, "Lord, I do not deserve to have you come under my roof. But just say the word, and my servant will be healed. ⁹ For I myself am a man under authority, with soldiers under me. I tell this one, 'Go,' and he goes; and that one, 'Come,' and he comes. I say to my servant, 'Do this,' and he does it." [10] When Jesus heard this, he was amazed and said to those following him, "Truly I tell you, I have not found anyone in Israel with such great faith. [11] I say to you that many will come from the east and the west, and will take their places at the feast with Abraham, Isaac and Jacob in the kingdom of heaven. [12] But the subjects of the kingdom will be thrown outside, into the darkness, where there will be weeping and gnashing of teeth." [13] Then Jesus said to the centurion, "Go! Let it be done just as you believed it would." And his servant was healed at that moment.

In verses 1-4, we find a leper kneeling before Jesus saying Lord, if you are willing, you can make me clean.

Let's look at this. First, he's a leper- an outcast. Lepers were considered unclean. They were supposed to keep their distance and were not welcome among the majority population but we find this outcast, unclean, unwelcome leper asking Jesus to help him.

This tells us that no matter who you are, what stigma you may carry and what issue seems to have a hold on you, you can still ask the Savior to help you.

Just because you are considered an outcast by people doesn't mean that you're out of reach to God!

Here's the proof! The bible said that Jesus reached out His hand and said, "I am willing, be cleaned." So not only did Jesus do just what he asked, He also touched him.

Beloved, the Lord is willing to make you clean. He's willing to make you whole and to make you free but the key to all of this is that the leper ASKED!

In verses 5-10, there are several things the Lord wants us to see.
1. Unselfish asking/requests: I'd like to pose these questions to you. Can you ask the Lord to help someone else? My second question is - will you ask? Are you willing to take a step into

34

the realm of *unselfish asking* where it has nothing to do with you and may not be of any benefit to you? I encourage you to ask the Lord to help someone else. Petition the Lord on behalf of somebody else. The Lord wants you to look beyond yourself, take the focus off of you sometimes and sow some seeds into someone else. That seed will only cost you some time, your attention and faith to believe for someone else.

2. Specific asking: The Centurion said "but just speak the word only and my servant will be healed." God said to share with you that it's alright if you ask Him specifically for you what you need or want. The bible declares that you are to make your request known unto the Lord (Philippians 4:6b). Jesus said ask and it shall be given (Matthew 7:7). He also said whatsoever you ask in my name, it shall be done (John 14:13).

3. Jesus wants to see your faith: You asking and Him answering has nothing to do with who you are or are not or what was done or not done.
   a. Look at Verse 9. The centurion runs down the list of what he has, what he does and who he is. Yet with all of that, he still asked the Lord for help. So essentially the Centurion was asking, if with his mouth, he could speak words and people move and obey and things happen, how much *more* can the word of God spoken by God accomplish?

The Lord sent me to encourage you to ask Him to help you. He just wants to see your faith.

Faith and healing are tied up in your ability and willingness to ask. Whether you ask for yourself or someone asks for you.

The answer to the question - can you ask God to help you is yes you can! I'd like to leave you with a challenge. *Will you ask the Lord to help you?*

Remember, you can ask the Lord to help you. You must believe that

He's willing and able to help you. And in between knowing and believing- ASK.

I challenge you to action. ASK! Show Him your faith and what you need will show up!

Prayer: Precious Jesus, my prayer today is that You will help me to put aside all pride and come humbly to You and ask for what I need. Lord, help my unbelief and help me to believe without doubting that You are able to do all things in my life. Lord, I thank You in advance for being willing to help me and I receive Your answers to my problems, healing for my hurt and Your redemption for my life. Thank You, God, that even though things may look dead right now, because I'm asking and believing in Your power, I know that You will help every dead looking area of my life. Lord, I'm ASKING and waiting for Your answer. In Jesus Name. Amen.

Day 7
Unseen Potential:
It's not as bad as it looks

Reference: Ezekiel 37:1-9 NIV

The hand of the LORD was on me, and he brought me out by the
Spirit of the LORD and set me in the middle of a valley; it was full of
bones. ² He led me back and forth among them, and I saw a great
many bones on the floor of the valley, bones that were very dry. ³ He
asked me, "Son of man, can these bones live?" I said,
"Sovereign LORD, you alone know." ⁴ Then he said to me, "Prophesy
to these bones and say to them, 'Dry bones, hear the word of
the LORD! ⁵ This is what the Sovereign LORD says to these bones: I
will make breath[a] enter you, and you will come to life. ⁶ I will attach
tendons to you and make flesh come upon you and cover you with
skin; I will put breath in you, and you will come to life. Then you will
know that I am the LORD." ⁷ So I prophesied as I was commanded.
And as I was prophesying, there was a noise, a rattling sound, and the
bones came together, bone to bone.⁸ I looked, and tendons and flesh
appeared on them and skin covered them, but there was no breath in

them. ⁹ Then he said to me, "Prophesy to the breath; prophesy, son of man, and say to it, 'This is what the Sovereign LORD says: Come, breath, from the four winds and breathe into these slain, that they may live.'"

In the thirty seventh chapter of Ezekiel, God is giving us an illustration of the promise from the thirty sixth chapter. The promise from chapter thirty six was to rebuild and restore the nation of Israel both physically and spiritually. In verse one of chapter thirty seven, the dry bones represent Israel. They are described as scattered and dead with no life in them and no hope.

Some of you are like these bones - scattered, lost and dead. Your spirits are broken, cast down and in some instances dead but as God promised, He will restore you with His word.

Ezekiel had a potential army lying before him but without the Word of God, the bones were just a form of what they could be. That's exactly what we are without God and His Word.

Let's look at some points that you can get from Ezekiel today.

1. Sometimes you have to be alone with God. Sometimes you have to be alone in the middle of your valley season. Often times you can't see or hear what God wants you to see or hear when you are with the crowd and in the midst of the happenings. Sometimes it's necessary for you to be in a place that looks like nothing is happening.

The good part about **unseen potential** is that it's not always what it looks like and definitely not always what you think. Sometimes you have to encounter the place that appears to be dead, appears to lack progress and appears to even deny your very promise just so God can show you what He really wants you to see.

2. Confessing your conditions. It's a matter of acknowledgement. Verse two of this lesson says "He led me back and forth among them and I saw a great many bones on the floor of the valley, bones that were very dry."

What do you see lying around on the floor of your valley? What appears dry? What looks dead? Where do you see lifelessness? Where do you feel hopeless? Look at your stuff, your valley full of bones, dreams that you let die, your spiritual walk that you let become stagnant, finances that look depleted or maybe your marriage that looks over. What are the bones that you need to speak to?

There is a word from the Lord - *it's not as bad as it looks*. That's just a form of what it could be. What you see is potential that is waiting on God's power.

Here's a key to developing *unseen potential*.

Look at verse four. We must hear the Word of the Lord. Stop listening to everything and everybody. Yes, the Lord speaks through the men and women of God and yes He uses them but sometimes it's got to be you, God and His Word. If you listen to the Lord, He will help you. If you hear the Word of the Lord, you'll hear your destiny, you'll hear your purpose, you'll hear clear instructions and you'll hear what He's planning to do for you. God wants you to know that what looks dead is about to come to life.

Here's another key from verse seven. You must say what God tells you to say, the way He tells you to say it. You must also do what God tells you to do, the way God tells you to do it and watch what happens. The proof is in what Ezekiel said in this verse, "and as I was prophesying…." As you begin to speak and do what God says- at the same time the power of God starts doing what He said He would do.

Simply said: While you're speaking, God is working!

If you'll make up our mind to speak as God speaks and do what God says, you'll look around and what you thought was gone or what looked like nothing will start taking form. The picture that you saw would have started to change right before your eyes.

Even more encouraging is what God said that He's going to do the further we read into these verses. He said after He's done raising you up, He's going to make you live! He's going to breathe life back into you. He's going to cause you to flourish and prosper.

Don't worry; *it's not as bad as it looks*. There is *unseen potential* that God is going to unlock in you.

Prayer: *Father, help me to lay aside my worry and believe what You say. Help me to see beyond what I see in the natural and know that You have the power to bring Your Word to pass. Lord, I pray that I will begin to work as You speak and that I will follow Your command as You speak. Although my situation may look bad, thank You Lord, for seeing the potential in me and breathing on me. In Jesus Name, Amen!*

Day 8
Dreamers Keep Dreaming

Reference: Genesis 37:5-11 NIV

Joseph had a dream, and when he told it to his brothers, they hated him all the more. [6] He said to them, "Listen to this dream I had: [7] We were binding sheaves of grain out in the field when suddenly my sheaf rose and stood upright, while your sheaves gathered around mine and bowed down to it." [8] His brothers said to him, "Do you intend to reign over us? Will you actually rule us?" And they hated him all the more because of his dream and what he had said. [9] Then he had another dream, and he told it to his brothers. "Listen," he said, "I had another dream, and this time the sun and moon and eleven stars were bowing down to me."
[10] When he told his father as well as his brothers, his father rebuked him and said, "What is this dream you had? Will your mother and I and your brothers actually come and bow down to the ground before you?" [11] His brothers were jealous of him, but his father kept the matter in mind.

"Dreams are forever until you decide to give up and stop dreaming."- Mo Stegall

What are dreams? Are they the images that often come to us when we are sleeping? Are they the ideas, thoughts and aspirations that we may have in our waking hours?

I believe that dreams are pictures, plans and blueprints drawn from the Master's view. They are those things that, until revealed to us, only God has seen.

These dreams may be what Paul referred to when he said eyes have not seen, ears have not heard, neither has it entered into the hearts of man the things which God has prepared for them that love Him.

Dreams could be depicted as those things that are exceedingly and abundantly above all that you could ask, think or image.

Unfortunately, dreams are the very things that you are allowing to fall by the wayside. You're giving up, fainting, throwing in the towel, aborting the missions and forfeiting the blessings.

The Lord said to encourage the dreamers and the visionaries. Whatever you do, don't stop dreaming and keep your eyes on the vision! You must stay focused on what God showed you.

Don't be distracted by the right now! Don't be distracted by what's behind you or around you. Focus on forward and *keep dreaming*.

Don't let your haters hinder you. Know this: Everybody is not going to accept you or your dream. Everybody is not going to believe in you or your dream. Everybody is not going to consent or cosign with you about it but *KEEP DREAMING*!

Don't even let your family hinder you. Just as Joseph's family was clearly against these great dreams that God showed him but He still had to live them. Don't miss that! Regardless of who may be against your dream, *you still have to live it*!

Joseph was thrown in the pit by his brothers and he had to live it. He was lied on by employer's wife but he had to live it. He was lied on by his employer's wife but he had to live it. He had to be thrown into prison but he had to live it. He had to be forgotten by his cellmates but he had to live it. He had to live all of that so that he could live the dream.

You might have to go through a pit season where it looks like you might die but you will live because you have a dream that must come to pass. You might be lied on by people but you will live because you have a dream that must come to pass. You might even go through a period of life that looks and feels like bondage but you will live because you have a dream that must come to pass. And it is almost certain, that the very people that you helped will quickly forget about you but don't you dare turn around. Don't you dare give up! You have a dream that must come to pass.

The enemy is going to try everything possible to destroy your dream. People may even envy it and your situations will make you want to forget it but *KEEP DREAMING*!

Distractions and disturbances will always come before destiny! But the destiny will come!

No matter how long the dream takes to manifest, we must learn to be like Joseph's father and keep the matter on our mind. Jacob may have rebuked Joseph but he kept the matter on his mind. Keep your dreams on your mind even if no one else has it on theirs. Keep the dream on your mind, in your eyesight and on your lips. Don't you let the enemy make you afraid to speak of your dream! Don't let the enemy silence you with fear! *Keep dreaming* and speak on it!

When the haters come, *keep dreaming* and speak on it! Even when the rebuke comes, *keep on dreaming!* When the lies get started, *keep dreaming* and speak on it! When others don't believe, you must keep believing! *YOU* must *keep dreaming*!

The time that it takes for it to happen doesn't change what God said. The opinions of people does not change what God said. The circumstances and situations that you may find yourself in do not change what God said. Remember that your dreams are your visual

God-saids. Your dreams are your blueprints. Your dreams are God's plan for you.

Don't let the lack of resources cause you to give up. Don't allow the lack of people supporting you to cause you to turn back. God is the God *of* the resources and as long as He's with you, you are never alone!

I can tell you from personal experience that there was a time that I allowed what people said and thought stop me from dreaming and moving forward. I was worried about what they thought, if anyone would buy the books or support the events but God said ***don't stop dreaming***.

You must believe that it is not what man says but the word that God spoke over your life that will come to pass. It is the dream He planted in you that He wants to manifest right before your eyes. It's the vision that He allowed you to see that will carry you past people's opinions. Beloved, what God said will happen.

And here is your proof – The bible teaches us that God is not a man that He should lie. If the Lord spoke it- it shall come to pass. He is not slack concerning His promise and He watches over His Word to perform it.

Yes, sons and daughters of God, you must ***keep dreaming***! God will do just what He said that He would do!

You must hold fast to what God has shown you. Get a firm grip on what God has confirmed in you.

When it's your time *and* your turn, the dreams and visions that you see will come forth.

The Lord wants to know - whose report are you going to believe? Whose opinion really matters to you? Whose view really counts to you? What power do *they* have to bring God's promise to pass?

All power belongs to God and He's able to perform every word that

He has spoken concerning you.

Beloved, God wants you to know – *"the place that you are in right now is just the place that you are in right now." (Bishop-Elect Brian J. Macon, Sr.)* It is not where you are going to end up. You will go where God said that you will go! You will do what God said that you will do! You will be who God said that you will be! Do *NOT* be distracted by right now. Right now is just right now, there is more to come!

Dreamers, you must keep dreaming! You must not give up! Don't allow anyone to distract you from your dream. Don't allow any negative report to outweigh what God has said to you. Your dream will live. Your vision will come to pass. You will have life and life more abundantly. You will obtain the promise. It's still secure. It's still sure. It's still valid and God is *still* going to do it. ***Keep dreaming***! It's coming!

Prayer: Precious Father, forgive me for every dream that I've given up and stopped working toward. Lord, help me to pick up the word that You spoke over my life and believe Your report for what's to come for me. God, help me to see my dream so that I can see my dream. Help me to stand fast only on what You have spoken. Lord, I believe You today and I believe that this dream and vision is from You. Because it's from You, I know that You will bring it to pass. Today, I make a commitment to get back to work on the dream You've given me and to keep working until You manifest it. I give You glory, honor and praise for reigniting the fire in me to work the vision and live the dream. Thank You for entrusting me with this dream. Help me, Lord, to work it in a manner that gives You all the glory. In Jesus Name, Amen!

DAY 9
WHAT'S STORED UP IN YOU?

Reference: Matthew 12:35-37 Proverbs 18:21 Job 15:6 NIV

Matthew 12:35-37 - A good man brings good things out of the good stored up in him, and an evil man brings evil things out of the evil stored up in him. [36] But I tell you that everyone will have to give account on the day of judgment for every empty word they have spoken. [37] For by your words you will be acquitted, and by your words you will be condemned."

Proverbs 18:21 The tongue has the power of life and death, and those who love it will eat its fruit.

Job 15:6- Your own mouth condemns you not mine, your own lips testify against you.

Beloved, I have some questions to pose to you concerning your choices for your life.
What are you storing up in you? Are you storing up the Word of the Lord or the wickedness of this world? Are you storing up the good things, the pure, the right, the lovely or are you storing up the hurt, pain, fear, brokenness, or feelings of uselessness, devastation and

46

resentment?

Even more so, who are you associating with that is depositing into you both positively and negatively? Who is the source that is combating all of the good things that have been poured into you? Who is your ungodly influence?

Too often most people want to revel in those positive people around them but *not* deal with the negative ones. When I say deal with them, I mean that you are allowing the negative people or things too much access to you. They have access to your eye gates and your ear gates. Your hearts are not guarded properly, your spirits are uncovered and as they deposit into you, you are storing up and holding onto these things that essentially begin to hold you down.

You have given too many wrong people a 'Yes' and not enough 'No's'. Your eyes are too focused on what they do. Your ears are trained to listen to their words. Your hearts are opened to someone who is not supposed to be there. Now you're singing that old familiar song- *how did you get here?* The simple answer to that is that you let them in!

You have opened doors that should not have been opened. You have granted permanent access to temporary people. You've allowed seasonal people to access lifetime luxuries. In short, you've created ungodly soul ties that could very well have been or will be deadly. If not physically, certainly spiritually, emotionally, mentally and often times financially as well.

Unfortunately, the bad has been more prevalent than the good. Some of you are carrying so much of the bad that it is outweighing the good. For all the good that you've done for people and toward them, it is the bad things that have happened and have been said that you remember because it's living in you. Now, sadly, it's coming out of you. Even worse is that the bad that is coming out far outweighs the good.

Not only that - what we've received via these deposits is now being repeated from your very own mouths. What they have said to you and about you, is what you're saying. You don't realize that it doesn't look or sound like anything that God has said about you. The bottom line is that you have too much of their word stored in you and not enough of God's Word.

Sometimes you may wonder why you say some of the things that you say or do some of the things that you do. It's time to check your internal storage compartments; look back at your deposit slips. You need to check out *who* has deposited *what*. Then check out what you received and what you allowed. Some of these things are *in* you simply because you allowed them. You didn't want confrontation. You didn't want to hurt anyone. But all of it was hurting you.

Whatever is coming out of you, whether it's good or bad, is only coming out because it's in you.

You may have heard some people say - that is so out of character for me or I'm shocked at that person. I would have never expected that from them but you never know what's been stored up in a person.

Truth be told, sometimes you've missed or overlooked what's been stored in you. Now it has set up residence in you and there is evidence because there is residue being sprinkled in every part of your life.

Think about how it is when you walk in a room and you instantly know that this certain person is either there or has been there. Everywhere you look, you see their stuff and no matter how many times you put the stuff up, it always seems to reappear. God said that's because you are trying to put it up and it's time to put it out!

This is your opportunity to change two things: What's stored in you and what comes out of you.

First, you have to acknowledge and address what's in you. Some of you already know what's stored in you. You know what's lingering, what's locked up in the old places of your hearts but you have chosen to overlook it. You bypass those things for the nicer, prettier, sweeter things of life.

God gave me this one prophetic word for the people- Deal with what's inside of you before it comes out of you and destroys not only you but also someone else. Examine yourself and confront the man in the mirror. Take off the faces that you've worn to cover up the things you wanted hidden. Open up those secret compartments in your heart and your life that need to be emptied out. Now, take a leap of faith and pour them out at the Master's feet and allow Him to pour into you the love, the peace, the joy, the goodness and more that He has stored up for you.

Prayer: Precious Father, I come to You humbly asking You to help me pour out everything that has been negatively stored in me. Lord, I ask You to help me release it and leave it with You. Help me not to pick up the old ways, old habits or old ways of thinking and talking. Thank You, Lord, for causing me to evaluate the things that have been left in me and the things that I've allowed in me. Lord, thank You that I now realize that what's going on in my life is a result of what's operating in me. Lord, thank You that today I can release these hindrances to You. I give them all over to You, Lord. I ask You to cleanse me of every ungodly soul tie that has been created in my life as a result of wrong relationships.

Free me, Lord, so that I can live for You. Free me, Lord, so that my negative experiences are no longer my issue but deliverance is my testimony. Lord, thank You, that on this day I give ALL of me to You. Lord, help me to store Your Word in me every single day of my life. Lead me to the word that You have for my daily bread. I pray that every day, I'll have more of You and less of me and less of others.

Lord, I thank You In Jesus Name! I believe this to be done in my life. Amen!

DAY 10
THE UNLIKELY CANDIDATE

1st Samuel 16: 1-3 & 10-12 NIV

1 The Lord said to Samuel, "How long will you mourn for Saul, since I have rejected him as king over Israel? Fill your horn with oil and be on your way; I am sending you to Jesse of Bethlehem. I have chosen one of his sons to be king." 2 But Samuel said, "How can I go? If Saul hears about it, he will kill me." The Lord said, "Take a heifer with you and say, 'I have come to sacrifice to the Lord.' Invite Jesse to the sacrifice, and I will show you what to do. You are to anoint for me the one I indicate."

10 Jesse had seven of his sons pass before Samuel, but Samuel said to him, "The Lord has not chosen these." 11 So he asked Jesse, "Are these all the sons you have?" "There is still the youngest," Jesse answered. "He is tending the sheep." Samuel said, "Send for him; we will not sit down until he arrives." 12 So he sent for him and had him brought in. He was glowing with health and had a fine appearance and handsome features. The Lord said, "Rise and anoint him; this is the one.

In this story, David is anointed as king. The first thing you need to know is that before Samuel ever laid eyes on David or anointed him with oil, God had already chosen him. Although his father Jesse had not even considered him, God had already chosen David. The decision was already made when God spoke to Samuel and gave Him instructions.

This is a reminder that even though people may have counted you out, God still had you on His mind. Even when you weren't even considered by others, you were already God's chosen vessel.

All of David's brothers had been brought before the man of God yet David was not even invited. When it was asked if there were any other sons, David was called in as afterthought. The Message Bible shows his father Jesse describing David as a runt. He was seen as *just* the one who was tending the sheep.

Let me interject right there that it doesn't matter what they call you when God has called you. It doesn't matter how they see you. They only thing that matters is how God sees you through His eyes. God looks beyond what people see and say. He looks beyond what you see and say and He sees what He said. God sees who He created you to be and what He designed you to do.

Undoubtedly, David was considered unlikely because he was a field worker but as a field worker he was trusted with his father's most valuable possession- his sheep.

Sheep represent those who belong to God.

So while no one else had given a second thought or look at David, God had entrusted to him that which He valued the most.

While David was working in the field, tending the sheep, guarding and protecting the sheep, he may *not* have *looked* like a King. His appearance may have been ragged because of the conditions that he worked in but he was still the chosen one.

David probably had the stench or the smell of the sheep on him because day in and day out he was working in the field but, beloved, God is looking for the ones who are doing the work. God isn't looking for the people who have titled up. I am not negating titles and mantles because it is an honor to carry a mantle in God's Kingdom. However, titles, mantles and positions mean nothing when there is no work that goes along with them.

Take a moment and evaluate what God has entrusted to you. You may find that you are already doing the work. Until now, you may not have realized that while you were working other jobs or helping others birth their visions, God may have been preparing you. I guarantee you that your work has not been in vain.

People may have even take you for granted and boxed you in based on what you've done for them but don't be discouraged. They could not see what God was planning for you or how they were a part of the preparation process. This could have been God's blessing in disguise to you. Can you imagine how David's brothers may have acted if they had known that David was going to be chosen over them? Sometimes it's necessary to be hidden. I'm sure that you remember Joseph's brothers. At the mention of Joseph's dream, they threw him in a hole. Beloved, if God has you hidden, it's really alright. It was really for your good.

You may have been working in the field all this time so that God could protect you until it was time for you and your assignment to be revealed. It's really okay if God allowed people to think of you as only a sheep tender, only a stay at home mom, only a part time writer or only someone that just sang at church. I'm sure they only thought of Rahab as a prostitute but she saved her whole family. Esther was probably seen as only a little orphan girl but she saved an entire nation. And Jesus was called- just the carpenter's son and He is the Savior of the whole world. Beloved, in God's timing, He will reveal that you *are* chosen and what you are chosen for.

It's actually very simple, beloved, God uses who He chooses. People can't *unchoose* you and they can't *uncall* you. It is what it is and you *are* God's choice. Just because you were counted as unlikely doesn't mean that God didn't choose you.

Maybe you are the one that is called for *this* season, *this* time, to slay *these* giants, to speak to *these* mountains or to put *these* demons to flight. Whatever your call, God said - ***you are the chosen one***.

You are chosen to work in *that* position and to carry *that* mantle. This was God's doing. It's time to stop being scared and timid and take your place.

You may be unlikely according to man but the Lord said **you're chosen**. You're waiting on man to approve you but God said that He has already done that. There is no undoing what God has already done. It's already written in His plan. Just because you *seem* unlikely does not mean you're not chosen.

The Lord is not swayed by man's opinion, by their looks and not even by the very gifts that He gave them.

You must remember God's Word- man looks at the outward appearance but the Lord looks at the heart.

The Lord said that He's not moved by any of what you see. He is moved by what He has already said and His word still reigns. He stands on his Word to perform it.

The Lord sent me to encourage you that even though it looks like you've been overlooked by man, chosen one, you can still take your place.

Because God is not swayed by people, you must not be swayed. When man tends to overlook you, your gifts and all that you can or do contribute to their lives, be encouraged, God has not overlooked you.

The work that you're already doing is preparing you for the work God has planned for you. When you feel rejected, be encouraged, God has already redirected your life. The rejection was allowed so that you would end up where God wants you.

When people don't think that you are enough, be encouraged, God has put enough *in* you.

You may not be man's choice but you must know that God has chosen you. Man's unlikely candidate is most likely God's candidate!

Prayer: Lord, thank You for choosing me! Thank You for the comfort of Your Word that reminds me that just because man may see nothing in me, You see

344443

what You made me to be. Lord, help me to release all of the feelings of being left out or rejected. I know that the enemy was using those things against me to keep me from seeing what You have for me.

Help me not to be swayed by the opinions of others but to live by Your Word. Thank You, Lord, for reminding me that people don't have to agree with Your choice of me for me to be chosen. Thank You for validating me and for reminding me that the seeds I've sown into others were preparation for the work You've called me to. Thank You, Lord, for changing the way I viewed these things so that now I can see You in all of them. In Jesus name, amen and thank God!

DAY 11
THE LORD WILL PROVIDE

Genesis 22:1-14 NIV

1 Some time later God tested Abraham. He said to him, "Abraham!"
"Here I am," he replied. ² Then God said, "Take your son, your only
son, whom you love—Isaac—and go to the region of
Moriah. Sacrifice him there as a burnt offering on a mountain I will
show you."³ Early the next morning Abraham got up and loaded his
donkey. He took with him two of his servants and his son Isaac.
When he had cut enough wood for the burnt offering, he set out for
the place God had told him about. ⁴ On the third day Abraham
looked up and saw the place in the distance. ⁵ He said to his servants,
"Stay here with the donkey while I and the boy go over there. We will
worship and then we will come back to you." ⁶ Abraham took the
wood for the burnt offering and placed it on his son Isaac, and he
himself carried the fire and the knife. As the two of them went on
together, ⁷ Isaac spoke up and said to his father Abraham, "Father?"
"Yes, my son?" Abraham replied. "The fire and wood are here,"
Isaac said, "but where is the lamb for the burnt offering?" ⁸ Abraham
answered, "God himself will provide the lamb for the burnt offering,
my son." And the two of them went on together. ⁹ When they

reached the place God had told him about, Abraham built an altar there and arranged the wood on it. He bound his son Isaac and laid him on the altar, on top of the wood. [10] Then he reached out his hand and took the knife to slay his son. [11] But the angel of the LORD called out to him from heaven, "Abraham! Abraham!" "Here I am," he replied. [12] "Do not lay a hand on the boy," he said. "Do not do anything to him. Now I know that you fear God, because you have not withheld from me your son, your only son." [13] Abraham looked up and there in a thicket he saw a ram[a] caught by its horns. He went over and took the ram and sacrificed it as a burnt offering instead of his son. [14] So Abraham called that place The LORD Will Provide. And to this day it is said, "On the mountain of the LORD it will be provided."

Beloved, the message for today is - don't worry, *the Lord will provide*.

The Lord said that He had to test your faith in a different way. He had to stretch your faith in the unfamiliar. It is often easy to be with the people and the things that you know but He had to pull you outside of your comfort zone. He had to get you out of the easy place and pull you beyond what you already know.

For the people who are in the place that God called you to, He said-don't worry He is your provision. If you're wondering how to know if you're in the place that God has called you to, you will know because it will not cause you to sin against Him. God will not call you to a place that will not glorify Him.

If you're in a place that contradicts His word, be assured that He didn't call you to it. He didn't send you to that. For the people who know without a shadow of a doubt, God called you to *this* mountain, the Lord said - don't worry, He will provide.

This place that you're in that feels or even looks unfamiliar- the Lord said don't doubt it. He has called you to it and because He called you to it, He will provide for you in this place.

If you have failed to move into the places and the things that God has called you to because of fear or because of lack of finances or resources- it's time to move. The things that you are concerned about or worried about are unnecessary. Sometimes you don't get the provision until you walk into the vision. You have to learn how to move on God's Word alone. It's time to stop waiting on everybody to be in place and all the money to be there. You're wasting time. The time to obey is now.

Many of you are consulting with this person and that person but you must look at Abraham's example. God spoke- Abraham moved. Am I negating wise counsel? Absolutely not, there is wisdom in multiple counsel but in some cases, in most cases, you must not delay your response to God's call. A delayed response could be a delayed blessing.

Look at what Abraham did- in verse 3. It says that early the next morning, he got up, gathered his things, his servants and his son and he head to the place that God told him to go. On his way, he encountered the mountain which represents the things and places that look larger than what you can handle. The mountain represents the things that you're not sure you can get over and things that you don't really know your way around. In plain language, he encountered that place that you've been called to but you don't quite know what to do or how to do it.

So Abraham went to the mountain and the next thing he did was hold on to his faith. We know this by what he said. He told the servants, stay here, the boy and I are going to worship and we will be back. So I ask you today- what is your faith saying? While you're looking at the bills, the relationships, the church, the mountain above you - what are you speaking? Are you speaking life or death? Abraham didn't say I'm going to go up here and slay my son and I'll be back. No, he said, *we* will be back. Beloved, you've got to have an "I'll be back mentality." He must have remembered the word of the Lord to him that said, you will have a son and call him Isaac and I will establish my covenant with him as an everlasting covenant for his descendants after him.

Isaac couldn't die because the promise wasn't fulfilled. You can't die because the promise that God spoke about you has not been fulfilled.

I challenge you to remember what God has already said to you.

Don't be so quick to forget God's promises when you see what looks like problems.

The Lord said, keep it in your mind that He called you to it!

Beloved, while you're on this journey, while you're in preparation to do what God has called you to, you must develop the testimony of Abraham. As he and Isaac were headed up the mountain, Isaac said to his Father, I see the fire and the wood but where is the lamb? Abraham's answer was- God Himself will provide the lamb.

We must trust that God Himself will provide everything that we need when we need it.

You may have big plans and ideas that you've written down. Maybe you've shared them with a few people but you're still wondering how it's all going to come together. God said to tell you – *He will provide.*

And let's look at Isaac. He didn't ask another question. When you understand that your provision is coming from God- all of the who, what, when, where and why doesn't matter, you just know- God is going to do it.

So I ask you today-Will you trust God without question? Will you trust Him without hesitation or reservations? Will you move on His Word alone? Will you obey Him just because obedience is still right?

The bible goes on to tell us that Abraham kept moving forward with his preparation to sacrifice Isaac but before he actually slayed him, the angel of the Lord stopped him. He told him - don't lay a hand on the boy. He said now I know that you fear God because you have not withheld your son, your only son. It goes on to tell us that there was a ram in the bush which became Abraham's sacrifice and he declared *the Lord will provide.*

But the Lord didn't only provide him a ram to sacrifice in place of his son. He also declared a blessing over Abraham and his descendants and all nations on the earth because of his obedience.

Beloved, the Lord said that you should know that your obedience births blessings.

The blessings that you seek, the miracles that you need, those things that you've been earnestly seeking God for, the healing you need, the deliverance you need, children of God- the Lord will provide. He just wants your obedience to His word.

He inhabits of our praise, our worship, our adoration but He desires our obedience.

The key to unlocking your blessings, even your children's blessings is in your obedience.

Will you move at God's word? Will you trust that He will provide? Will you obey Him now?

You must get it in your spirit that obedience births the blessings of God.

There was also another Son that came into the world over 2000 years ago. That Son was Jesus. He came in obedience to His Father. He spoke in obedience to His Father. He lived in obedience to His Father. He died in obedience to His Father and He rose in obedience to His Father. Beloved, His obedience unlocked the blessing of salvation to you.

His obedience unlocked the blessing of grace and the blessing of His tender mercies. He tore the veil in two. He unblocked the blessing of direct communication with the Father. You can go to the throne, beyond the veil and into the holies of holies. You can bow before the King- the King of Kings.

Because of His obedience- now you're called the redeemed. The heavenly inheritance has been unlocked for you.

I wonder if you will finally obey the King? You keep saying God's got the keys. No, God's got the blessings. You have the keys- it's in your obedience!

Beloved, if you will take God at His word and believe Him today, you'll find out that He is a man of His Word. What you need, the Lord will provide. What He promised, the Lord will provide. What you ask for in His name, the Lord will provide. He's able to do just what He said and because He can't lie and His Word will never return void, you can be assured that the Lord will provide. In every situation, regardless of what it looks like, you can believe God- He will provide. Whatever you need, God has it and He is able to provide it for you.

I pray that you won't lose hope and give up. Don't give in to the negative thoughts that make you feel that you won't make it. Don't allow the enemy to rent space in your head that he can't pay for. You must believe that God will come through for you. Just as He provided for Abraham and pronounced blessings over his life, God is able to do the same thing for you.

Be encouraged and believe that the Lord will provide for you!

Prayer: Dear Lord, help my unbelief. I receive Your word but I need help to know that You will provide for me. Thank You, Lord, for showing me in Your word that You always have an answer for every mountain that I face. Lord, help me to obey You more. Help me to walk in complete faith of Your word and Your promises. I admit that I don't see how things are going to work out for me but help me to trust you more, Lord. Thank You, in advance Lord, for providing for me. In Jesus name, Amen!

DAY 12
CONVERSION NOT COMPLIANCE

Genesis 19: 17 & 26 NIV

17 As soon as they had brought them out, one of them said, "Flee for your lives! Don't look back, and don't stop anywhere in the plain! Flee to the mountains or you will be swept away!"

26 But Lot's wife looked back, and she became a pillar of salt.

Beloved, God is calling for His people to live in total conversion and not simply compliance. What does that mean? It means that God wants us to live for Him because we want to live for Him and not because someone has told us this is what we should do. He wants our lives to be freely given to Him.

To be compliant means to give in easily; to follow the rules because they are the rules or to do what you were told just because you were told.

To be converted means to be changed, to be transformed; for the condition to be changed, not the same.

God wants you to be converted and not just in compliance. No longer will you simply follow the rules because those are the rules, you'll follow them because you love the ruler. That signifies change.

Compliant living is to do what you're told but like Lot's wife looking back to your real desire.

But changed, converted living is doing what God says and not looking back at what He called you away from. It is not thinking about what you were losing or leaving but just being focused on what God said do and where God said go.

When you are simply living in compliance, you may be doing something begrudgingly and not wholeheartedly.

When you are converted or changed, your obedience comes from your heart. You will take no thought of anything else but doing what God said.

God wants more than compliance from you. He wants you changed. You must stop looking back. What's behind you must be left alone.

At the beginning of every year, many people begin fasting. Most people participate in the 21 day Daniel fast. The issue is that you're fasting because this is what the Pastor has called or this is what you do every year and that is compliance. God wants you to be converted. Conversion will cause you to fast with the purpose of being changed, transformed, renewed, and being strengthened.

The Lord said that He's moving you from mere compliance to conversion. He's changing *you*. You may want God to change your situation but God said that He's changing you. You may feel like you have changed but God said there's more to do.

Luke 22: 32 from the Message Bible says: when you have come through the time of testing, turn to your companion and give them a fresh start.

There is a purpose for your change. God needs you to be converted so that someone else can be converted.

After this time of testing and when you have been renewed, God said it will be your turn to renew someone else.

He's converting you so that the condition of your heart will change. He's removing the heart of stone and replacing it with a heart of flesh.

You will no longer reach back just because that's what you're supposed to do. You'll reach back because you will want someone else to receive what God has given you. That's the change in your heart that God wants you to receive.

Conversion is definitely different from compliance. Compliance is simply because it was said to do it. It's what people see on the outside. Conversion is a matter of the heart.

Remember 1st Samuel 16: 17- "But the Lord said to Samuel, Do not consider his appearance or his height for I have rejected him. The Lord does not look at the things man look at. Man looks at the outer appearance but the Lord looks at the heart."

People of God, the Lord wants to change your heart.

Although you've grown from the place that you used to be, God wants to grow you some more.

Lot's wife went because she was told to go. She looked back because that's not what she wanted to do. She complied temporarily and partially.

Lot went because He was told to go. With a different heart and mind, he kept going and never looked back. He believed what the angels of the Lord told him.

Conversion causes you to take God at His word.

As you submit to the will of God and the word that He has spoken to you, watch Him change your heart, your mind, your talk, walk and life.

Beloved, God wants you to be converted not just in compliance.

As I close this article, I'm reminded of an old song sang by Tremaine Hawkins called *Changed*. The lyrics simply say -*Changed- I'm so glad He changed me. A wonderful change has come over me. He changed my life and now*

I'm free. He washed away all my sins and He made me whole. He changed my life complete and now I sit at His feet to do what must be done. I'll work and work until my Savior comes. A wonderful change has come over me. He changed me, I'm so glad He changed me. I'm not what I want to be, I'm not what I used to be, I'm not the same anymore. I'm changed.

I want to encourage you today to surrender your life to Christ. Allow Him to convert you so that you will receive the blessings that are attached to living completely for Him. The compliant life may render minimal blessings and rewards but why settle for the minimum of God when you could experience the maximum of Him. Remember that converted people move and live from a place of love for God while compliant people only do it because they are told to.

What will be your testimony? Converted or Compliant; it's your choice.

Prayer: Precious Father, I thank You for allowing me the opportunity to choose complete conversion over partial compliance. I pray that You will forgive me for my lack of obedience to You and for half-heartedly serving You. Lord, in every area of my life that I've served You out of compliancy, forgive me. If there are areas that I don't realize I've done it, show me. Help me to live in complete conversion and submission to Your will. Thank You for the precious blood that was shed for my conversion so that I could live freely in You. I freely give my life, my mind, my heart and soul to You. Thank You, Lord that today is a day of change for me that will show up in the way I live and love from this day forward. I'm depending on You, Lord, to continue to show me the right way to live converted for You. In Jesus name, Amen!

DAY 13
THE PROMISE IS STILL YOURS

Habakkuk 2:2-3 NIV

2 Then the Lord replied: "Write down the revelation and make it plain on tablets so that a herald may run with it. 3 For the revelation awaits an appointed time; it speaks of the end and will not prove false. Though it linger, wait for it; it will certainly come and will not delay.

Beloved, I would like to offer you some words of encouragement. Often times God will speak something to us and as time passes we grow weary because we have not seen what was said. Today, take a moment and revisit what God has said to you. If you have not written down the visions and dreams that God has promised you, now would be a good time to do so because He wants you to know that the promise is still yours.

The word that God spoke over you is true. Whatever God has said *about* you, it is still true.

God said there is something that He wants you to do while you anticipate the manifestation of your promise.

1. Write the vision. I urge you to write down the revelation and/or vision that God gave to you. Whatever God promised you, whatever He showed you about you, write it down. Write it down in detail. Don't leave anything out, not even the smallest detail. Even if the details seem silly to you, if God said it, write it. Habakkuk said to make it plain. However God said it to you, write it just like that.

2. You must remember that the vision is for an appointed time. Don't get anxious because you feel like it's been too long or you've gotten too old. The Lord is a promise keeper. What He has shown you and said to you is pointing you to what is coming. You must keep believing and you must be prepared.

With that said, consider these questions as you revisit your visions. If it manifested today, would you be ready to receive it? If it showed up today, would you be able to walk in it? Would you be ready or getting ready?

God said that now is the time to get ready for the appointed time.

Your vision will not prove false according to God's Holy Word. It will not lie. You will not be deceived by it and you will not be disappointed. God said that this is not a setup for failure but you will succeed. You will succeed if you do it His way. You will succeed if you prepare yourself now for the vision that He has shown you.

Don't throw in the towel now and don't turn around.

Just because you have not seen it yet does not mean it's not coming.

Just because what you see right now does not line up or look like what you heard and saw does not mean that what you heard isn't coming.

This is what Habakkuk said - though it tarry- meaning though it linger, when it looks like it's not going to happen, when the progress slows down – the prophet Habakkuk said wait for it.

Stay in faith and keep believing!

You won't have to manufacture it. You won't have to coerce or create it. He simply said wait for it. It will come and when it comes, it will not delay.

So while you're waiting, don't get discouraged. Prepare yourself.

While you're waiting, don't give up - get ready.

While you're waiting- Work! Always remember that your waiting time is your working time.

The Lord said that whatever He has said to you, about you and for you, He is going to do it.

Whatever He promised, He's going to bring it to pass.

Beloved, the Lord said that the promise is still yours. There is still a vision for you. It's on the way now and it will surely come.

You must get ready. You must believe that God is able to do just what He said that He would do.

Be encouraged because the favor is still resting on you.

If you are waiting on your promise to come through, now is the time to write it down and make it plain. Commit it to the Lord in prayer and work while you believe God to bring it to pass.

I'll encourage you as the song sang by *Darwin Hobbs* says- *Exceedingly, abundantly above all you could ask for according to the power that works in you - God is able to do just what He said He will do. He's gonna fulfill every promise to you. Don't give up on God cause He won't give up on you. He's able.*

Believe that for yourself today! Exceedingly and abundantly above all you could ask for and according to the power that's working in you. Don't give up. The power of God is working in you. You can still live your dream. You can still accomplish those goals. Beloved, the promise is still yours!

Prayer: *Dear Lord, thank You! Thank You so much for reminding me that the promise is still mine and that You are able to bring it to pass. Today, Lord, I vow to write down the vision You have given me for my life, my home, my marriage, my business and more. Today, I stand in faith and believe You without doubting that every promise that You've made me, You will keep it. Thank You, Lord, for being a promise keeper. Thank You, Lord, for not giving up on me. Thank You, Lord, that every promise according to Your Holy Word, will come to pass. I praise You in advance for what You're about to do. I praise You in advance for the visions that will come to pass. Thank You, Lord, that I will be able to live my dreams. I make the declaration over every vision, dream, and plan that you've spoken to me that You are able to do just what you said and I'll work while I wait for You to bring them to pass. In Jesus name, Amen!*

DAY 14
GOD'S INTENTIONAL DELAY

John 11:21-22; 40 NIV

²¹ "Lord," Martha said to Jesus, "if you had been here, my brother would not have died. ²² But I know that even now God will give you whatever you ask."

⁴⁰ Then Jesus said, "Did I not tell you that if you believe, you will see the glory of God?"

Delays are something that most people can relate to. You may remember praying about a specific situation or problem and feeling like the answer was never going to come. Maybe you were in a season that you thought would have been different if the Lord would have just answered you faster.

God wants you to know that just because He did not answer when you wanted Him to or the way you wanted him to, does not mean that He won't answer. It just means that there is something more that He wants you to learn from the experience. There is a purpose in your life for everything including the delays.

Let's examine the story of Lazarus. God wants to deal with things that look dead or delayed in your life. More importantly, He wants to address your requests that seem unanswered; those things that you have put before the Lord and it appeared that God either didn't answer or that He didn't answer on time.

You will remember in the story that Mary and Martha sent a message to Jesus that Lazarus was sick. When He received the message, Jesus replied saying that this sickness would not end in death. He said that this was for God's glory so the son of God may be glorified through it.

And then - Lazarus died.

Have you ever prayed for something, gotten an answer from God and then what happened next did not look like what God said?

Lazarus's story teaches you to listen carefully to what God says. Every word that He speaks is important to you believing Him wholeheartedly. It also indicates that only one word spoken over your life could make the difference.

In Lazarus's case, it really didn't matter if Jesus actually showed up on the scene because He had already spoken the final word over His life. He spoke a word that we often overlook when reading this passage. He said this will not *END* in death.

God said to tell you that it won't END like this. It only looks like it's over but He has already spoken the final word concerning you. This is just a delay. It is not a denial.

I'm talking about your *THIS* - your situation, your business, your project, your marriage and so forth. God said that He has already spoken concerning your "IT."

Just as He said to Martha at the grave, didn't I tell you that if you believed, you would see the Glory of God? Jesus also said in His prayer to the Father that He said this for the benefit of the people standing there, that they may believe that God sent Him.

Beloved, The Lord had to delay His answer for your benefit. Your waiting period was allowed so that you would learn not to waver when the Lord speaks to you. It was to move you to a place that you would believe what He has *already* said. What Jesus spoke about Lazarus is also true about you. It will not end in death! In other words, it's going to live.

I dare you to get your *IT* in your mind and start declaring what the Lord said - it's going to live.

Your vision may look dead. Your project may look buried. But in the words of Jesus, it will not **end** in death. It's going to live!

It is imperative that you believe what God has said. Even when you are standing at what looks like the grave of your situation, you must believe. If you believe, the promise is that you will see the glory.

The Lord said that although this delay was intentional, it was not allowed to hurt you but to help you. It was not meant to break you down but to build up your faith in Him.

God wants you to know that regardless of what happens around you or to you, you can still believe His word concerning you. Regardless of what looks like it's *not* going to happen, you will still be able stand firm knowing that if the Lord said it, it will come to pass.

While you've been crying over what you thought you lost, God has already declared that it will live.

Your dream will live. The barriers between you and the glory of God have been removed. You can stand firm on your faith and trust what He said about you. Not only are the things in your life going to live but so are you.

Even though it *looks* like it's over; that's not what He *said*. And because it doesn't look like what God said, you can be assured that it's not going to **END** like this.

Your IT has to do what He said, says the Lord. Your issue has to obey His command. Your problem has to line up with what God said the resolution is.

In the words of Jesus, didn't I tell you if you believe, you will see the glory?

Jesus said to tell you, people of God, it will live. This was only a delay. He allowed the delay to help you. He allowed the delay to build you up. He allowed the delay to strengthen you. He allowed the delay so that you would believe and so that you could see His glory.

Whatever your IT is, IT will live. He may not have answered you when you thought He should have. The answer may not have come in the manner that you thought it should have. It may not have even come through the resource that you expected but His answer will always be right and always be at the right time.

It's time to cast aside your fears and doubts because what the Lord has spoken concerning you will manifest. Beloved, if God said it, you can look for it. You can expect it. You can depend on it. When God spoke it, He put His name on the line. He put His reputation at stake so be assured that He will do just what He said. Don't focus on the delay of your answer. Don't worry that you haven't gotten the answer that you wanted when you wanted.

Now is the time to focus on what God said and believe that you will receive it. You could be in a season of delay but what you have requested of the Lord has not been denied.

Prayer: *Dear Lord, help me to hold on during the delay. Thank You for reminding me that every delay is not a denial. Teach me what I need to learn from this experience. Show me what I may be missing because I was focused on what I wanted. Lord, thank You that your timing is always right and whenever You answer me, however You answer me, it will be right. Forgive me, Lord, for not believing what You've already spoken about me. Help me to live in expectation of Your word coming to pass concerning me. Thank you, Lord, that this season of delay is only a delay and what You have planned for my life will come to pass. Thank you that I will learn more about me, more about others and more about You in this delayed season. Thank you, Lord! I will see the glory of God in my life because I will believe You. In Jesus name, Amen!*

DAY 15
MORE BLESSED THAN YOU THINK

Matthew 5:3-12 NIV

³ "Blessed are the poor in spirit, for theirs is the kingdom of heaven.
⁴ Blessed are those who mourn, for they will be comforted. ⁵ Blessed
are the meek, for they will inherit the earth.
⁶ Blessed are those who hunger and thirst for righteousness, for they
will be filled. ⁷ Blessed are the merciful, for they will be shown mercy.
⁸ Blessed are the pure in heart, for they will see God. ⁹ Blessed are the
peacemakers, for they will be called children of God. ¹⁰ Blessed are
those who are persecuted because of righteousness, for theirs is the
kingdom of heaven. ¹¹ "Blessed are you when people insult
you, persecute you and falsely say all kinds of evil against you because
of me. ¹² Rejoice and be glad, because great is your reward in heaven,
for in the same way they persecuted the prophets who were before
you.

Beloved, you are more blessed than you think you are.

While you're considering what a true blessing is and counting your more tangible blessings - materials and possessions, jobs and family - you should consider what Jesus said and see how blessed you really are.

Looking at what Jesus said about being blessed will change the very standard by which you measure a blessing.

The first thing that Jesus says is that when you're at the end of your rope with less of you, there is more of God and His rule. That alone is an immediate blessing to have more of God.

At the moment that you're ready to give up because it appears that everyone is against you, everything that could happen wrong is happening, remember that more of you and less of me is more than a song. Jesus said that's when you're blessed.

If you're finally at the end of you and your desires, you are in the blessed place. If you're feeling like you can't go on the way that you've been going, you are in the blessed place. The place where you end is where the blessings of God and His purpose begin.

Beloved, God wants you to live in the blessed place.

In the blessed place, you may feel like you've lost what is most dear to you. God wants you to see that the Uzziah in your life that was blocking your view of God had to be removed. Now that it's gone you'll draw nigh unto God and it will cause Him to draw nigh unto you. When that happens, that's when you're in the blessed place.

When you have become comfortable and confident in who you are- you don't have to down play yourself or puff yourself up. Jesus said that you're blessed because you finally realize that what you have *in* you can't be bought with money but only given by God. This is the blessed placed because you're good with what you do have and don't have. You also realize that what you have is more than what you don't have and it's really what you need.

Jesus said that you're blessed when your appetite is for the things of God; when your satisfaction comes from drinking at His fountain.

When you're not pulled away by the lights and glamour of this world but your real sincere delight is in Him, Jesus called that the blessed place.

The blessed place are those times when you show mercy when mercy is not your only option. It is the times that you don't necessarily feel like mercy is deserved but you give it anyway. When you do this, you are in the blessed place and because you show mercy, mercy will intervene for you.

Jesus also called us blessed when our hearts remain pure toward Him. This is when your motivation is advancing the Kingdom and not yourself. This is when you'll keep working regardless of your outward conditions, circumstances or issues. It's the blessed place when your aim is to live for Him in your circumstances and with your issues just because you love Him and nothing else.

We are blessed when we can show God's people how to cooperate instead of compete or fight. There is no fight for a place or a role in the Kingdom because God has already assigned and designated your place. Our job is to work together. People of God, our gifts were given to us to complement one another. Scripture teaches us that we are many members but one body. We were meant to build one another up, not tear each other down.

The Kingdom is calling for cooperation not competition.

Beloved, if you're being persecuted, picked on or put down-Jesus said count yourself as blessed. Every time anyone does those things to you, remember Jesus words- the least that they've done unto you, they've done unto Him and in the blessed place—vengeance is mine saith the Lord, whatever is right I will repay. It is a blessing to know that God will fight your battles.

The next time the enemy attacks you, remember that Jesus called it a blessing. How so? It's not about you. Satan is really trying to tear down the things of God. It's a blessing because there's something about you that is an eternal threat to the kingdom of Satan and you're blessed because this battle is not yours. The spirit of God that is living in you is warring against the attacks *and* the attacker on your behalf.

So the next time you're looking for or attempting to count your many blessings, remember what Jesus said:

The Kingdom of heaven is yours. You will be comforted. You will inherit the earth. You will be filled. You will get mercy. You will see God. You will be called the Sons of God and great is your reward in heaven.

So people of God, when you're counting your blessings and naming them one by one, remember what Jesus calls a blessing. Don't overlook something because you don't like it. Don't forget something because it doesn't feel good. Many of us are living in the blessed place already and don't even know it.

I challenge you to readjust your views on blessings. Reconsider the tests and trials of your life and remember what Jesus said. Rejoice and be glad. You are more blessed than you think.

Prayer: *Lord, thank You for helping me to readjust my views of what being blessed really looks like. Thank You, Lord, for helping me to understand that my blessings are far beyond these things that I can touch and see but I am blessed in the things that I've lived through. Glory to Your name, Lord, for the trials, tests and tribulations because now I see the blessing in them. Lord, help me to always remember that all things work together for my good because I love You and I'm called according to Your purpose and because of that, I can see all things as a blessing now. Lord, I pray that as I grow in You, I will be more like You and that I'll learn to embrace every area of my life as a blessing because it was allowed by You. In Jesus name, amen!*

Day 16
You can't lose

Mark 10:29-31 Message Bible

29-31 Jesus said, "Mark my words, no one who sacrifices house, brothers, sisters, mother, father, children, land—whatever—because of me and the Message will lose out. They'll get it all back, but multiplied many times in homes, brothers, sisters, mothers, children, and land—but also in troubles. And then the bonus of eternal life! This is once again the Great Reversal: Many who are first will end up last, and the last first."

What a promise from the Lord that - you can't lose. Despite what it may look like and regardless of how things may appear to be going right now, Jesus said that you can't lose.

Specifically Jesus said, "*Mark my words,*" in other words- remember what I'm telling you because it's going to happen. Whatever you have sacrificed, given up or walked away from for Jesus and the Gospel, Jesus promised: 1. You will not lose out, even if you feel like you're losing right now. 2. You will get it all back! Multiplied, many times.

Whatever you gave up - get ready to get it back. Get ready to get more because more is looking for you. The Lord said that you must remember His word—Give and it shall be given, good measure, pressed down, shaken together and running over shall I cause men to give unto your bosom. God is preparing people to bless you.

Let's look back at the scripture - it says that they'll get it all back, multiplied many times in homes, brothers, sisters, mothers, children and land- BUT ALSO IN TROUBLES.

I know that you may be worried about that clause that said *but also in troubles* but you've got to look at how Jesus handled the "troubles" in this teaching. He didn't dwell on that one statement. That teaches you to be aware of it but don't dwell on it. That's a strategy for you. Be aware of the trouble, you can't ignore it, but you cannot dwell on it.

When you begin to get it all back as Jesus promised, trouble will come but don't dwell on it.

When what you have sacrificed is multiplied back to you, trouble will show up but don't dwell on it.

God is saying don't let the trouble overshadow your triumph. You can't lose!

You are winning because if God be for you who can be against you? You are winning because If God be for you, He's more than the world against you. Who can stand before you when you call on that great Name?

You've got to know that after the troubles, there's more to come. You may ask- how will you know? This is your assurance. Jesus said *and the bonus of eternal life.*

Every time you see trouble, remind yourself that there's more to come. Every time you feel hard pressed, remind yourself that you're not crushed - there is more to come. When you're perplexed, remind yourself that you're not in despair - there is more to come. When you're persecuted and you *will* be persecuted, remind yourself that you're not abandoned because there is more to come. When you're struck down, remind yourself that you are not destroyed because there is more to come. When the enemy comes in like a flood, remind yourself that the Spirit of the Lord will lift up a standard against him and there is more to come.

God knows what you gave up seems great and you feel like you don't even know what's next but He said to tell you that MORE is next! There's more good coming to you. There is more of what you've given out coming back to you.

Don't dwell on the trouble. Don't dwell on what you're losing or letting go of because there is more to come. Don't dwell on what you see right now because it's not the end. One thing may be ending but this is not the end for you. Don't dwell on the obstacles- Jesus said you can't lose. Don't dwell on the lack because plenty is coming and you can't lose.

God said He's got much for you and then He's got much more. I love the way the Message Bible read- it says this is the Great Reversal. The first shall be last and the last shall be first.

Get it in your mind and spirit today that God is turning it all around for you.

Whatever you lost, count it as gained. Whatever you sacrificed, count it restored. Everything that looks bad right now, take another look because He is turning it around for you. Everything that feels bad, don't give up on it just yet - He's turning it around for you.

People of God, Jesus said that you can't lose.

Your labor has not been in vain. Your praying and fasting has not been in vain.

Galatians 6:7-9 in the Message Bible says this- *Don't be misled: No one makes a fool of God. What a person plants, he will harvest. The person who plants selfishness, ignoring the needs of others—ignoring God!—harvests a crop of weeds. All he'll have to show for his life is weeds! But the one who plants in response to God, letting God's Spirit do the growth work in him, harvests a crop of real life, eternal life. So let's not allow ourselves to get fatigued doing good. At the right time we will harvest a good crop if we don't give up, or quit.*

I love the part that says *But the One-* Beloved, the Lord told me to tell you that you are the one! You are the one that has planted in response to God. You have moved when he said move - just like that. You have sown when God said sow. You have prayed when He said pray. You have stood in the gap, you have been the midwives and now God is saying that You are the one that He will do the growth work for. You are the one that He will multiply it back to. You are the one that will get the reward in this present age, you're going to see the goodness of the Lord in the land of the living and then you're going to get more.

Don't get tired now. Keep doing what you're doing! Now is not the time to give up on you and losing is not an option.

Keep preaching the word, keep serving in your church, keep interceding for others, and keep obeying the voice of the Lord. Whatever the Lord has assigned to your hands, keep doing it. Be instant in season and out of season because you already know that you can't lose.

Keep doing it - when you feel like it and when you don't. Keep doing it when people are listening and when they're not. Keep doing it when you see results and when you don't. Keep admonishing. Keep rebuking. And Pastors, preachers, and leaders, keep preaching holiness because holiness is still right. Whatever you do, don't stop because you can't lose.

Beloved, service is your ministry. Keep serving because your service to God's people is your service to God and you can't lose serving God.

Keep interceding. Praying without ceasing is your charge. Never stop praying because the fervent, effectual prayers of the righteous availeth much. The *more* that's already looking for you is going to show up while you're praying.

Remember Peter - while they were yet praying, God had already answered.

There is an assignment in your prayers. Somebody will be covered by your prayers. Somebody will be delivered by your prayers. Somebody will be healed and set free. While you're praying, the chains are falling off of you and somebody else.

Beloved, your labor is not in vain and you will not go unrewarded. Even when it looks like no one sees, God sees you. He sees your work. He sees your heart. He sees your sacrifice.

Don't abandon your post. Great is your reward, says the Lord. The Lord has not forgotten about you and His word is still true concerning you.

Hold on just a little while longer. Your due season is closer than you think.

Hold your position. Keep standing and after you've done all to stand. Stand!

It was not in vain! You can't lose! You were born to win! You were persecuted so you'd have power! You were alienated so you could be anointed. You were broken so you could be useful but in all of that - you can't lose! Whatever state you're in right now, you can't lose! Paul said it best - for we KNOW all things work together for the good of them that love the Lord and are called according to His purpose.

People may have counted you out. They thought that it was over for you. Surely you couldn't recover from this hurt, this pain, this break up or this job loss but overflow is coming, increase is coming and abundance is coming.

You are about to walk into the time of exceedingly and abundantly. You're about to experience what eyes have not seen, what ears have not heard and the things that have not even entered into the hearts of man! You're going to get it back, multiplied many times! They thought that you were dead, but you can tell them I'm back! They thought it was over but God has said NOT SO!

Your anointing is authentic.

The bondage is broken off of you.

The chains couldn't hold you.

The chaos is canceled.

Your deliverance is here.

Your future is secure.

Favor is on you.

Grace is overshadowing you.

Mercy has intervened.

The Lord told me to encourage you to remember that it is IMPOSSIBLE TO LOSE while we are serving the God that makes ALL THINGS POSSIBLE!

So run and tell that, You can't lose!

You're not going to walk in fear. You're not going to be intimidated! You will not back down. You will not shy away. You're not going to play small. You're not going to dummy down. In fact, you're not going to be able to because you're about to get it all back and then some!

They are questioning your gift, they are questioning your call, they even watched you fall but you're still about to get it all back. They have seen you suffer but now they are about to see you reign.

I double dare you to run and tell that - you can't lose. I heard the spirit of the Lord saying its coming and before I take it back I'll add more to it. This is the season of manifestation and it will come. You can't lose with what God has given you to use. Use your power. Use your anointing. Use your brokenness. Use your prayer. Use your pitfalls. Use your purpose. Use your worship. Use His Name. His name is Jesus and Jesus said -You can't lose.

They saw you lose it all, now they're about to see you gain it all back. David said "you prepare a table before me in the presence of mine enemies." They were watching you then when they thought it was over and please believe that they are watching you now. But what they're about to see is something they've never seen. You are more than just the comeback kid, you are a child of the King and King's kids can't lose.

Beloved, you're about to get it all back and then some! You've been setup for more and you will receive it. You may have had to sacrifice. You may have suffered some losses but what you're about to get back is not only going to bless you but it's about to silence them.

As we've heard it said many times before, beloved, you ain't seen nothing yet. Lift your head up, encourage yourself in the Lord and prepare yourself to win because Jesus promised that you can't lose.

Prayer: *Precious Father, thank You Jesus that I can't lose! Thank you, Jesus, that whatever I thought was lost, You've already said it's coming back. Thank You, Lord, for speaking this word into my life. Lord, I receive Your word and I believe it to be true concerning me. I decree over my life that losing is not an option. I decree that I will win because You are for me. Thank You, Lord, that even when I was counted out, You counted me in. Glory to Your name, Father that I belong to you. Glory to Your Name, Lord! I believe that my best is yet to come*

. Thank you, Lord Jesus, for the authority to use what You've given me and to stand firm on Your word. I receive it in my heart today Lord and I will wait in expectation to receive everything that You have promised. In Jesus name, Amen.

DAY 17
IT'S TEMPORARY

John 16:20-22 NIV

^{20} Very truly I tell you, you will weep and mourn while the world rejoices. You will grieve, but your grief will turn to joy. ^{21} A woman giving birth to a child has pain because her time has come; but when her baby is born she forgets the anguish because of her joy that a child is born into the world.^{22} So with you: Now is your time of grief, but I will see you again and you will rejoice, and no one will take away your joy.

Beloved, I want to offer a word of comfort and consolation to you. I want to remind you that God is very aware of everything that you are enduring right now. Be encouraged because after all this, God is going to turn your grief into joy. This place and time is only temporary.

Most times when you hear the word grief, it is associated with the death of someone. However, there are so many areas in our lives that we could be grieving.

You may be grieving the loss of a loved one. You may be grieving the loss of a relationship or marriage. Some people are grieving the loss of a job and the results of it. You're grieving everything that seems to be lost because of your loss. You may be grieving the loss of status, positions, and maybe even possessions but God wants you to know that this grief, this pain and these times are only temporary.

You may have even lost some things, people or a job by no fault of your own and you are dealing with the residue of what happened. Be encouraged because in a little while, there is a turnaround coming for you.

God knows that it looks like the whole world is rejoicing around you. It seems like everybody else's life is just going on happily while everything is changing for you. Everybody else's life seems to be stable but you are weeping and mourning. God said that this isn't a season of reaping; it's simply a part of the process. Some things just have to happen.

This process was to get you from the place you were in to the place where you are now. And this place that you're in now is to prepare you and propel you to where He wants you to be.

The statement "this is only temporary" may be comforting to some people. However there are others who are asking - how long is temporary? The answer really is as long as it takes. Your temporary is as long as it takes for you to be pruned. It is as long as it takes for you to be purified. It is as long as it takes for you to be processed. *As long as it takes*. That's how long temporary is.

But there is good news. It will turn around for you. Jesus used the example of a woman giving birth to describe how He will turn your grief into joy.

In that process, He talks about the pain that a woman experiences because her time has come. You are experiencing so much pain right now because your time has come. You are experiencing so much pain right now because your time has come. The good news is that the pain is about to cause you to give birth to your joy.

Beloved, God wants you to know that He has given you the strength to push through the pain.

We all know that labor times and pains vary from one woman to the next. There is no set time for labor to begin or end. Labor begins when it's time and it ends when it's time. Most times, there isn't an exact date of birth given. The doctor gives the mother an expected date of delivery.

Beloved, I have to encourage you concerning the pain that you are experiencing right now. You have an expected date of delivery. The word of God teaches us that many are the afflictions of the righteous but God will deliver you out of all of them. You can EXPECT for God to bring you out. You can EXPECT for these trials, tribulations, problems, illnesses and so forth to come to an end.

This is labor time for someone and God wants you to push through your pain. You may feel tired, you might be weary but this birthing process will bring your joy. The process carries you through your pain and to your joy.

You are entering into the time of turning and God is starting with your grief. He's turning it into joy.

Your pain is not only becoming praise but it is becoming your purpose.

Everything that you've been in, you'll work harder to pull other people out of. What you've experienced, you'll use it to speak life and deliverance to somebody else. Everything you gain as a result of what you thought you lost, you'll use it to bless someone else.

God said He's turning it around, starting with your joy and it's happening in just a little while.

The Lord said He's going to turn your grief into joy. He's going to erase the anguish of the pain that you're going through.

He knows that the grief and pain has felt unbearable at times but He's going to wipe out the very memory of this pain.

God said that He's got to get rid of all the old stuff because when He turns this thing around for you, you must have room to receive what's coming! You had to go through it to get out of it.

Jesus said in verse 22- NOW is your time of grief but I will see you again and you will rejoice and no one will take away your joy.

People of God, I pray that you will receive the promise of God. Even NOW during your time of grief, when you're feeling like every day is a press to get up, a press to get moving - receive what Jesus said to His disciples for yourself. Push your way through this pain because Jesus has promised that you will rejoice.

Don't give up now. Don't stop moving forward. After all this, no one will be able to take your joy away. This is just a temporary time in your life but the turn around that Jesus promised IS coming for you.

Prepare yourself for the morning! The weeping has endured and just as God promised, the joy has to show up.

Prayer: Lord, I come to You thankful that You are working behind the scenes on my behalf. Thank You Lord that even though I feel like my troubles are unending, You have promised that You will turn them around for me. Lord, I pray that every obstacle in my life is turned around according to Your word. I pray that every hindrance in my life is turned around according to Your word. Lord, help me to stay strong while You work out the issues of my life. Lord, help me to push through my pain and grief and hold on to Your promise that joy is coming. I thank You in advance that the turnaround for my life is on the way. I thank You and I rejoice because I take You at Your word Lord and I know that it will come to pass. In Jesus name, Amen!

Day 18
Don't Be sidetracked
by the distractions

Luke 11:17-28 NIV

Jesus knew their thoughts and said to them: "Any kingdom divided against itself will be ruined, and a house divided against itself will fall. ¹⁸ If Satan is divided against himself, how can his kingdom stand? I say this because you claim that I drive out demons by Beelzebul. ¹⁹ Now if I drive out demons by Beelzebul, by whom do your followers drive them out? So then, they will be your judges. ²⁰ But if I drive out demons by the finger of God, then the kingdom of God has come upon you. ²¹ "When a strong man, fully armed, guards his own house, his possessions are safe. ²² But when someone stronger attacks and overpowers him, he takes away the armor in which the man trusted and divides up his plunder. ²³ "Whoever is not with me is against me, and whoever does not gather with me scatters. ²⁴ "When an impure spirit comes out of a person, it goes through arid places seeking rest and does not find it. Then it says, 'I will return to the house I left.' ²⁵ When it arrives, it finds the house swept clean and put in order. ²⁶ Then it goes and takes seven other spirits more wicked than itself, and they go in and live there. And the final condition of that person is worse than the first." [27] As Jesus was saying these things, a woman in the crowd called out, "Blessed is the mother who gave you birth and nursed you." [28] He replied, "Blessed rather are those who hear the word of God and obey it."

Beloved, this article was written to encourage you when you are faced with distractions. In Luke 11: 17-28, Jesus was talking (teaching & preaching) except for verse 27 when all of sudden a woman calls out "Blessed is the mother who gave you birth and nursed you." A distraction.

Distractions are a direct attack of the enemy against the word of God and the things of God that you have been called to do.

Distractions often halt something that you are doing or to throw you off track and cause you to lose your focus.

Distractions are meant to make you miss what God is doing or is about to do in your life. They cause you to lose focus on what God is doing through you and for you in the Kingdom in the area that you are working in.

Distractions sometimes come to shake your faithfulness and make you question if what you're doing is really the right thing.

And distractions come in all forms, shapes, things and most certainly in the form of people.

The woman that yelled out as Jesus was teaching was a potential distraction to Jesus and to the hearers. If allowed to continue, she would have distracted them from what He was teaching and building by His Word.

The way that Jesus responded lets us know that distractions will come. They may have to be addressed but they don't have to be effective in our lives. Distractions don't have to stop you.

Jesus simply replied, "Blessed rather are those who hear the Word of God and obey it," and moved on.

It was an answer that continued to instruct the hearers and simultaneously dismissed the woman that attempted to cause the distraction.

Beloved, you must learn to follow Jesus example when distractions come. You must keep doing what you were sent to do. Don't dwell on distractions and don't allow them to throw you off track.

The Lord said don't question where He has put you. Don't question the things God has set your hands to and whatever you do, don't take your hands off of it.

Even when you have to address your distractions, don't stop working. Something happens when you stay the course.

You can be encouraged by verse twenty-nine. It says *"as the crowd increased."* If you properly handle your distractions, you can experience increase despite the attack to cause havoc or interrupt you. You must be careful of how you handle your distractions. How you handle them may determine how your next phase reads.

Ask yourself these questions: Will your response to an attack or a distraction draw an increase or cause a decrease? Will you continue working when the little things that appear big begin to pop up? Will you be able to discern that they are distractions, address them and move on?

The Lord said that He has called you to this assignment. Now is not the time to give up. You must keep doing what you're doing.

Too often people give up on themselves and the things that God has assigned them to do because of distractions. Even more often, we hold onto the things that we should have let go of long ago which is also a form of being distracted.

Now is not one of those times that you should be giving up too soon or holding on too long. Beloved, NOW is not the time to be distracted. This time and your assignment are too critical.

Not only is this your assignment but this is also your service. Remember that your service to Gods people *is* your service to God. Whatever you give out in the Kingdom, you are giving it unto God.

Don't abandon your post. Great is your reward, says the Lord. Don't stop serving, don't stop studying and don't stop praying.

Be like Jesus and hold your position. Keep standing and after you've done all to stand. Stand.

Your labor is not in vain. You must suffer with Him to reign with Him. The hymn writer said *"must Jesus bare the cross alone and all the world go free, no there's a cross for everyone and there's a cross for me."*

Beloved, this distraction that you're encountering now, this place that you're in right now, this feeling that you're enduring right now - it's just a part of the cross. But after the cross was victory. After the cross was Glory.

Don't be sidetracked and don't give up now. The Lord said that you should remember where He brought you from. Not only the place that He brought you from but the YOU that He brought you from. You're not that person anymore and you don't belong in that place anymore. You've come too far from where you started from.

I say this scripture often because I believe it to be true. For I reckon that the sufferings of this present time are not worthy to be compared with the glory which shall be revealed in us.

Beloved, don't be distracted, don't give up - there will be glory after this.

Prayer: *Dear Lord, forgive me for the distractions that I have allowed to stop me from working. Help me to identify the distractions in my life and work through them. I commit all my work to You and decree that I will keep working the assignments that You have given me. I acknowledge that I've given too much attention to things that are not as important and allowed them to stop me. I ask You to help me to focus more on You and Your Word. Thank You for Your example of how to handle the distractions of life. Help me to follow Your lead and keep going even in the face of distractions. Lord, I pray that the distractions of my life will be rebuked in Jesus name. I pray that they will no longer be a hindrance to me. In Jesus name, Amen!*

DAY 19
WHAT HAPPENED TO YOUR SEED?

Galatians 6:7-8 NIV

Do not be deceived: God cannot be mocked. A man reaps what he sows. [8] Whoever sows to please their flesh, from the flesh will reap destruction; whoever sows to please the Spirit, from the Spirit will reap eternal life.

At certain times of the year, particularly around holidays such as Thanksgiving and Christmas, there tends to be a lot of love expressed; a lot of caring and even more giving and receiving. Typically parents go all out with the gift giving to their children, families share in gift giving and everybody is excited to receive. But beyond these seasons, there is giving and receiving that takes place that often goes overlooked.

There are times that you feel like all you do is give, give, give and never or hardly ever receive. You tend to question the seed and harvest time. You find yourself wondering - when will your time come? When will that time come when all the sowing and giving yields a return? You may be wondering will there ever come a time when somebody will pour into you? And the truth is that you really don't care to hear - *it's not your season* - not one more time.

The Lord said if you are wondering what happened to your seed, you may want to check the way you threw it and the ground that you threw it into.

Look at what the scripture says regarding how you sowed those seeds. In Galatians 6:8- For he that soweth to the flesh shall of the flesh reap corruption but he that soweth to the spirit shall reap life everlasting.

God said it's time for a self-assessment of yourself and your seed. Not just money but time, talent, gifts and anointing.

Why did you sow what you sowed? Why did you sow it to who you sowed? Did you sow it for your own benefit? Did you sow it because you liked the preacher? Did you sow it because you loved the person? Did you sow because you felt like that was your friend, your person or whoever and this is what we do? Did you feel like you've got each other's back and they would do the same thing for you?

Or did you sow to the glory of God? Did you sow with a heart that said God I just want to bring you glory? Did you sow and nobody knew? Did you sow to be pleasing to God out of obedience to His word?

God understands that you want to know - what happened to your seed? It's time to ask yourself-WHY?

The second thing is what kind of seed did you sow? 2nd Corinthians 9:6 says remember this- whoever sows sparingly will also reap sparingly and whoever sows bountifully will also reap bountifully.

Did you give your best seed or did you just throw in what was left? Did you give God your best fruit, your first fruit or just a portion of what may have been left over?

Was that seed your bare minimum just for the sake of saying you gave or did you give from the abundance of the blessings God has given you?

When you sing, did you sing just because you can or was it for the glory of God?

When you preach, was it just because you think you can or was it for God to be glorified and the people to be edified?

When you teach, was it just because somebody said you can or did you really want to share the revelation knowledge that God so freely shared with you?

When you gave, was it to get your name on the top ten givers list or was it simply because God, this is what is required?

You're wondering what happened to your seed and God said - YOU did!

The last thing that God wants you to evaluate is where you sowed those seeds. Where you've sown sometimes resembles the picture described in Matthew, chapter thirteen.

Some of your seed fell by the wayside. It never even made it into the ground because it was snatched up.

Some of your seed fell on stony ground. It looked like it sprang up quick as if you had gotten a quick return, but then just as quick it was gone because it had no roots. There was no depth to it.

Some of your seed fell among thorns. It grew up and then it got choked out. It didn't last.

But some of your seed fell on good ground. The bible says that the good seed brought forth fruit. It produced a crop but for those who didn't and you are wondering what happened to my seed- the Lord said, be encouraged, there is news about your seed.

There is bad news and there is good news.

Look at what the words says: Galatians 6:7- the bad news is that whatsoever a man soweth THAT shall he also reap but the good news is whatsoever a man soweth THAT shall he also reap.

So sometimes you find yourself in the season of "giving and receiving" yet you're wondering what happened to your seed?

The Lord said- where did you sow it? How did you sow it? Why did you sow it? What did you sow?

Whatsoever a man sows *that* shall he also reap.

If you sowed goodness, goodness is coming back to you.

If you sowed mercy, mercy is coming back to you.

If you sowed love, love is coming back to you.

Everything that you've sown, it's all coming back to you.

And if you sowed money, I decree that it's coming back to you. Oh, yes it will. Job 22:28 says that you will decree a thing and it shall be done unto you.

The Lord said in this season of your life, not the time of year, but in this season that you're in, now that you understand what has happened to your seed – God said that He's still honoring His word.

Whatsoever a man sows *that* shall he also reap.

God said, I made you a promise and I will keep it.

At the proper time, at the appointed time, you will reap a harvest if you faint not.

Beloved - faint not. Don't give out now. Regardless of what it looks like, you've got a seed in the ground and you've got to reap the harvest.

Stand firm and believe that it's coming back to you. Whatever you sowed, that's what you're going to get!

Prayer: Lord, make me ready to receive. Lord, I've sown the seeds and now I'm expecting a harvest. Lord, I know that some of my seeds may have been sown in the wrong places and maybe I sowed for the wrong reasons. Lord, I ask You to please forgive me. I thank You Lord for speaking life to me concerning my seeds and helping me to understand that I must be careful of where I sow, how I sow and who I sow into. I give You praise Lord, because now that I know better, I will do better. Thank You Lord for honoring Your word to me and giving me hope that I can still reap a harvest. In Jesus name, Amen!

Day 20
It won't drown you

Matthew 14: 22-32 NIV

22 Immediately Jesus made the disciples get into the boat and go on ahead of him to the other side, while he dismissed the crowd. 23 After he had dismissed them, he went up on a mountainside by himself to pray. Later that night, he was there alone, 24 and the boat was already a considerable distance from land, buffeted by the waves because the wind was against it. 25 Shortly before dawn Jesus went out to them, walking on the lake. 26 When the disciples saw him walking on the lake, they were terrified. "It's a ghost," they said, and cried out in fear. 27 But Jesus immediately said to them: "Take courage! It is I. Don't be afraid." 28 "Lord, if it's you," Peter replied, "tell me to come to you on the water." 29 "Come," he said. Then Peter got down out of the boat, walked on the water and came toward Jesus. 30 But when he saw the wind, he was afraid and, beginning to sink, cried out, "Lord, save me!" 31 Immediately Jesus reached out his hand and caught him. "You of little faith," he said, "why did you doubt?" 32 And when they climbed into the boat, the wind died down. 33 Then those who were in the boat worshiped him, saying, "Truly you are the Son of God."

Beloved, I want to remind you that God's got you!

In the midst of the contrary winds of your life, Jesus is near. You may wonder how is that so especially when it doesn't feel like it with all that you're facing. His word says that the Lord is close to the broken hearted and He saves those who are crushed in spirit.

People of God, even in this storm, the Lord is near you.

The scripture says "but the ship was now in the sea, tossed with waves, for the wind was contrary." When something is contrary, it's against you. It could also mean that it is unfavorable or adverse. However in the next verse it says, "Jesus went out to them walking on the sea."

The interesting part of this passage is that while the disciples were in trouble they didn't call on Jesus but He still showed up.

Even though the storm was raging, the conditions were unfavorable and the situation could have been considered adverse, Jesus showed up.

I want to remind you that when the situation looks bad, the storm is raging and adversity is at its worst, even if you don't call the Lord, He will show up to see about you.

Look at what happens when Jesus shows up. The word says in the midst of the storm, the disciples saw what they thought was a ghost and cried out. Jesus heard them and immediately started talking. He said, "Be of good cheer, It is I; do not be afraid."

Beloved, that is God's word for you. In the midst of this storm, be of good cheer, He is here.

He is saying to you like He said to Peter- Come! Walk out on the water with Him. Put your fears and doubts aside and come!

There is a call for you to come even with all that you have going on. Jesus is saying come! You want to wait until things get better, you're more financially stable, or until you have a team to help you but there is no time to wait. Jesus is calling you to come to Him now!

You want to wait until you get yourself together but Jesus said come!

You're worried about failure. You're worried that you won't be supported. You're worried that you won't have what you need. Child of God, take your eyes off of what is going on around you and put your focus back on Jesus.

Stop focusing on who isn't there and acknowledge and be grateful for who is there.

Remember Peter in this passage. Jesus said come and one translation says that Peter boldly got out of the boat and began to walk on water. He began to walk on the very thing he feared would drown him.

Beloved, Jesus is calling you out of your boat.

The things that you thought were going to overtake you - you now have the power to walk on at His command.

The master of the seas, the one who controls the storm even when it's raging is calling for you to come.

Beloved, you have the authority to walk on the things you thought would overtake you.

Abandonment can't drown you.

Broken heartedness can't drown you.

Chaos can't drown you.

Depression can't drown you.

Emptiness can't drown you.

Loneliness can't drown you.

Unforgiveness can't drown you.

Lack of finances can't drown you.

Ungodly relationships can't drown you.

Negative thoughts can't drown you.

Naysayers can't drown you.

Counterfeit supporters can't drown you.

Tricks and traps of the enemy can't drown you.

Hurt can't drown you.

Pain can't drown you.

Memories can't drown you.

Sin can't even drown you if you take that step and come to Jesus!

Jesus is saying come out of your boat because it won't drown you!

Prayer: *Precious Father, help me to trust You more. I admit that I feel like I'm drowning. Help me to believe that regardless of what it looks like, I won't drown. I come to You now, Lord, giving You everything. I give You my worries, my doubts and my fears. Thank You for keeping me from drowning even when I didn't know that You were keeping me. Thank You for protecting me and shielding me. Help me not to be afraid when things come against me or when I'm faced with hard trials. I believe that You will keep me if I come to you. In Jesus Name, Amen!*

DAY 21
THE ANSWER TO WHY

John 9:1-3 NIV

As he went along, he saw a man blind from birth. [2] His disciples asked him, "Rabbi, who sinned, this man or his parents, that he was born blind?" [3] "Neither this man nor his parents sinned," said Jesus, "but this happened so that the works of God might be displayed in him.

Many times as you experience trials and tribulations, you tend to ask the Lord – why? Often times that question comes from your feelings about a particular situation or it comes from what you see going on around you. Too often you look at other people's lives and wonder how they got blessed or why you are not blessed like them with the things that they have. We look for these reasons or answers in something wrong that we've done and most times we blame others as well.

The Lord wants to give you the true answer to - Why?

The first thing that the Lord wants to cancel in your life is the blame game. It's not always that something has been done wrong or someone has sinned. God wants us to know that some things were simply *allowed.*

You may be saying - but God that doesn't answer the question of *why* it was allowed. God said the answer to why rest in two words- The Glory.

The Lord knows that you are seeking an answer. You've been searching the record of your life, looking for the seed that you sowed that has caused you to be in this reaping season you're in. God said that's not where the answer lies this time.

Children of God, you have been tormenting yourself with a barrage of unanswered questions.
1. Why are you going through what you're going through right now today?
2. Why did the marriage fail after you did all that you could do?
3. Why did your business fail even after you followed the plan?
4. Why does it feel like you're suffering on top of suffering?

The Lord said that this is His Glory and how He gets it is not for you to decide.

There's a reason why your husband didn't, can't or won't find you in the way or the place that you thought he would.
There's a reason why your wife didn't or has not come in the way, shape or time that you planned, thought or wanted.

You couldn't get the job that you went to school for, planned and worked hard for at that time.

There's a reason that it seems like nothing that you planned has worked. Your plan had to fail so that God's plan could succeed. Remember His word-for I know the plan I have for you, plans to prosper you and not harm you, plans to give you hope and a future. (Jer 29:11)

The Lord said that He allowed these things to happen in your life, in this manner, so that when the Glory of God is revealed in your life-you nor anyone else's handwriting or finger prints would be found on this.

After this, you'll understand that it wasn't your good works, hard work or strategic planning. You'll understand that not even the people God put in your life could have done this but as the song says- *No one else can receive God's glory.*

For all of God's children who may be worried about what people might think or say, it doesn't matter. It doesn't matter if they question what happened or why. You have an answer from God. It's not even about you, it's about the Glory!

People of God, be encouraged because you have this promise - all things work together for the good of them that love the Lord and are called according to His purpose.

You have your answer to why- It's the Glory and God wants to get it out of you!

Prayer- *God, thank You for Your glory that will be revealed in my life. Thank You for Your hand that is evident in my life even when I don't recognize it. I bless You now that Your plan is succeeding for my life. I take no credit for the work that You are performing in my life. I am humbled before You that You would choose to use me. God, I don't take Your grace and mercy for granted but I thank you for another chance to serve in Your Kingdom. Father, I thank You that You are the source of my life and Your resources never run out. And God I thank You that in all things You are the answer. I thank You that as I decree a thing it shall be established. I plead the Blood of Jesus over every area of my life. Thank You that I am covered, protected and shielded. I decree the success of your plan in my life, the glory of God revealed, Your will shall be done and the good works of God shall be found in my life. I thank You. I love You. I praise You. It's in Jesus name that I pray Amen and thank You!*

Day 22
The Walls Have Got To Go

Joshua 6:1-5 & 16 NIV

Now the gates of Jericho were securely barred because of the Israelites. No one went out and no one came in. ² Then the LORD said to Joshua, "See, I have delivered Jericho into your hands, along with its king and its fighting men. ³ March around the city once with all the armed men. Do this for six days. ⁴ Have seven priests carry trumpets of rams' horns in front of the ark. On the seventh day, march around the city seven times, with the priests blowing the trumpets. ⁵ When you hear them sound a long blast on the trumpets, have the whole army give a loud shout; then the wall of the city will collapse and the army will go up, everyone straight in."

¹⁶ The seventh time around, when the priests sounded the trumpet blast, Joshua commanded the army, "Shout! For the LORD has given you the city!

I heard a message a few years ago from a brother in the Lord, Apostle Brian Little entitled "Been There Done That." During that message it was said that because of things that you've encountered and relationships we've been in we have declared - I've been there and done that, got a t-shirt and a testimony.

Often you may say that you have learned your lesson and won't be caught doing those things again. Essentially you have erected walls in an effort to protect yourself not realizing that the things that you're calling protection have now become blockages.

People of God, the Lord wants you to know that He is about to tear down the walls that are blocking you from what God wants you to have.

God is aware that you feel like you've gone as far as you can go. He knows that you feel like as hard as you try to move forward, there always seems to be something holding you back.

He hears you child of God that feels like the city of Jericho. You feel like your life is tightly shut up. It feels like nothing good, productive or lasting is coming out of you and even more you don't feel like anything is getting in.

It seems that no matter how much you have pressed your way to the house of God, nothing is speaking to you. Even when you're diligently seeking, you still can't seem to find that thing that you need for you.

What you've needed is closer than you think and it's not going to take God long. God is about to deal with the walls of Jericho in your life.

Jericho was a fenced town with high walls. It represents the high things in your life and the things that look out of your reach. The Lord said that He's about to put them in your hand.

In this text, after the Lord declared that He was giving them the land, He also gave them instructions on how to fully obtain what He had for them.

Whatever God instructs you to do - do it. Don't worry about who doesn't agree, like it or who doesn't understand. Don't you know that God uses the foolish things to confound the wise?

To confound means to perplex, to confuse or bewilder. It's a surprise or sudden disturbance. Can you imagine Jericho's surprise when the thing that they thought was their safety net, the thing that they thought couldn't be penetrated suddenly came crashing down?

Imagine their surprise when the access they thought they controlled was suddenly granted to outsiders *without* their permission.

God said He's about to give you access to places that you've been previously denied. He is even about to give you access to the places you've said - been there, done that. You've tried it on your own but they wouldn't let you in. He's about to give you access to people who otherwise wouldn't have associated with you. Your gifts are about to make room for you and bring you before great men.

Yes, the walls in your life must go!

There was also a time of instruction that Joshua said don't say a word until the day I tell you to shout. People of God, this is the day to shout because God has given you the city.

Don't miss what God is saying. He has given you the city.

The first thing you should know is that what He has for you, He has already done it. It's already yours.

The next thing that you should take notice of is that He said- the city.

A city is defined as something large, something important, usually governed by some other authority but beloved God said you're about to get *your* authority.

And here is what the Lord said for them to do.

When the walls come down, the people shall go up, every man straight in.

The Lord is saying to you, He's about to tear the walls down for you and you need to go straight in.

If your wall is your job, it's coming down.

If your wall is in your home, it's coming down.

If your walls are in your church, they are coming down.

If your walls are from a relationship, they're coming down. It's time to let it go and move on.

The walls of complaining must come down because you are called to worship.

The wall of insecurity, thinking that you're not good enough is coming down. You must remember that God uses who He chooses and because you were created by God, you are good enough.

The wall of negative talk is coming down. You will not talk yourself out of what God said. If the Lord said it, it's must come to pass. If he put you in that position, that place, with that person, then you are equipped for it.

If lack and poverty have been the walls that were blocking you, it's coming down. Increase is coming to you and so is the wisdom to know what to do with it.

If fear has been your wall, it's coming down. Jesus said fear NOT. God has not given you the spirit of fear but of love, power and a sound mind and you're about to use what God has given you.

People of God, the walls of your Jericho are about to come down and the Lord said go get it.

We must not only be hearers of the word but doers. Beloved, it's time to go up and go in and get it.

The walls have been brought down for you and the city has been given to you. It's time to use your authority and go get it!

I decree and declare that every wall in your life that has been blocking you is coming down in the name of Jesus. I decree that every wall that you've erected is being torn down in the name of Jesus. I decree that the Lord is dealing with your Jericho's and the walls that have held you back in the past will no longer do so. Beloved, you are free to go up, go in and get what God has released to you.

Prayer: *Lord, I thank You that my walls have come down. Thank You, Lord that everything that was holding me back is being handled by You. Thank You Lord that even the walls that I've erected trying to protect myself will no longer hinder me. I receive everything that You have for me. If I don't know what those things are then Lord I ask that You will show me. Show me where I need to go up. Show me where I need to go in. And teach me how to go get it. Thank You for blessing my life Lord and removing those things that I don't need. Help me to never erect walls or allow walls to be built by others that will hinder my life and keep me from what You have for me. I give You praise, honor and glory. In Jesus name, Amen.*

Day 23
You are free! Go!

Mark 5:25-27 & 34 NIV

And a woman was there who had been subject to bleeding for twelve years. [26] She had suffered a great deal under the care of many doctors and had spent all she had, yet instead of getting better she grew worse. [27] When she heard about Jesus, she came up behind him in the crowd and touched his cloak, [28] because she thought, "If I just touch his clothes, I will be healed."

[34] He said to her, "Daughter, your faith has healed you. Go in peace and be freed from your suffering."

In this season of your life, your objective should be at all times, in all circumstances, issues, decisions and even ailments- to get to Jesus.

When situations arise, God wants you to have a mindset to get to Jesus.

After you've emptied yourself out, untangled yourself from some bondage and strongholds, and become free, when things rise up - get to Jesus.

Beloved, something happens for you and *in* you when you get into the presence of Jesus. Wholeness, freedom and direction happen when you get to Him.

God wants you to know that your slate is wiped clean. You've got a fresh start. God wants you to go forth and live in your freedom!

Now that the shackles are off and the weights are lifted- God wants you to **go**.

It's just that simple, **Go**! Jesus has done the work in you.

I'm sure many of you reading this will say that it is easier said than done. That may be absolutely true but it shouldn't stop you from going.

God also knows that you have questions.

Where are you going? Seek the Lord in prayer and find out where He wants you to go.

What am I doing? Ask yourself, what did He tell you to do?

He has the answers to every question that you have.

If you'll seek the Lord, the bible teaches us that you will find Him. You can connect with Him beyond the veil. But while you're seeking, remember that His instructions are to **Go**!

Beloved, you may have been through hell but heaven has responded. Now it's your move! **Go**!

It's time for you to make some progress, even if it's one day at a time or one task at a time.

Can you imagine the woman with the issue of blood as she must have debated about entering the crowd to get to Jesus? She must have contemplated what people would say. She may have even feared what they might do considering she was an outcast because of her illness. Yet, she made up her mind to go. She made up her mind to get to Jesus. Maybe she decided that nothing was more important than getting to Him.

If you'll make up your mind to get to Jesus and put all of your fears and worries aside, you'll find that what you need is in Jesus.

God is saying that the season that you were in really is over. All you have to do is **go** and **be free**. **Go** and don't look back. **Go** and don't return to the places of bondage and sin that you've been in before.

The season of testing and preparation is complete. The season of discouragement is over. The season of confusion, disobedience, disorder, chaos, and crippling is over. It's time for you to **go** and do what you've been assigned to do.

Maybe this is your time to finish things that you started or start things that you've been procrastinating and not doing.

God is giving you a do over. All He wants you to do is **go**!

You can make a decision about what the tone of your life will be. You have the power to decide how well you will walk in your freedom. If you'll get to Jesus and follow His lead, you'll find that you're already free. Beloved, God is calling and it's time for you to **go**.

Prayer: *Lord, I thank You for complete freedom in You from every issue that had me bound. I lay everything at Your feet and choose to be free in You. Thank You Lord that I don't have to stay in the place that I was in or do the things I was doing. God, I have a made up mind to do what You have told me to and go where You have told me to go. Help me to walk in my freedom every day of my life. Show me where I need to go and what I need to do and help me to do it in complete obedience. I thank You, I love You and I praise You. In Jesus Name, Amen!*

Day 24
Do You Believe That
God Is Able To Do This?

Matthew 9:27-29

²⁷ As Jesus went on from there, two blind men followed him, calling out, "Have mercy on us, Son of David!" ²⁸ When he had gone indoors, the blind men came to him, and he asked them, "Do you believe that I am able to do this?" "Yes, Lord," they replied. ²⁹ Then he touched their eyes and said, "According to your faith let it be done to you."

This story is very short and seems very simple but it is really significant. It is a great example of faith in action. In these two short verses we find two blind men who are following Jesus and there are three things that we immediately know about them.

1. They could not see Jesus.

2. They knew that Jesus was there.

3. They knew that Jesus had what they needed.

The first thing that they teach you through their story is to follow

God even when you don't see Him in your situation. Follow God even if you can't hear Him speaking to you. Follow God even if you have times when you just don't feel Him.

It's really not about what you can see, hear or feel but it's about what you know.

Do you *know* like the blind men knew that He's there? You must always remember that He said He'll never leave you and He'll be with you even until the end of the earth.

Secondly, do you *know* that He's got everything that you need?

In verse 28- Jesus asked them the most important question - do you believe that I am able to do this? They answered, yea Lord!

I want to encourage you to know that He is able to do THIS!

What is *THIS*? It's whatever you need and God is able to do it.

He's able to build you. He's able to carry you. He's able to deliver you. He's able to grow you. He's able to hold you. He's able to love you. He's able to make you. He's able to save you. He's able to redeem you. And He's able to heal you.

My next question is - what is your *THIS*? The old preachers used to say- He's a lawyer in the courtroom who has never lost a case. He's a doctor who has never lost a patient. He's a mother to the motherless, father to the fatherless and friend to the friendless. He's salvation to the sinner and redemption to the captives. And He can free the bound.

This could be your peace in the midst of mayhem. *This* could be your joy in times of sorrow. *This* could be your help when you're in trouble. But whatever your '*this*' is - the blind boys said - He's able.

Jesus said to the blind men, "according to your faith, be it unto you."

Jesus was whipped, beaten and bruised. He was mocked, sneered at and spit on. He hung, bled and died and He rose. So now it's on you. Beloved, according to *your* faith be it unto you.

As you consider the things that you may be facing or the even the visions that God has given you, I only have one question for you - do you believe that He's able to do THIS?

Do you believe that He can heal you? Do you believe that He can save you? Do you believe that He can redeem you? Do you believe that He can sanctify you? Do you believe that He can justify you? Do you believe that He can even glorify you? Do you believe that He can make you new? Do you believe that He can renew you? Do you believe that He can restore you?

Beloved, be it unto you according to your faith. All you have to do is believe that God is able to do this for you and it will be done!

Prayer: *Lord Jesus, please help my unbelief. I know that You are able to do all things so please help me to believe You even in the hardest times. Lord, whatever You want to do in my life, do it for Your glory. Help me to follow You. Help me to know that You are with me even if I don't feel like it. Thank You for reminding me that You have everything that I need at all times. I pray in faith, believing that You will provide for me and that You will show up for me. I thank you in advance for what You will do. In Jesus Name, Amen!*

Day 25
The benefit Of
Taking Refuge In God

Psalm 34:8 NIV

Taste and see that the LORD is good; blessed is the one who takes refuge in him.

Many of you are hiding in many places, from many things because of various reasons yet you have no peace, no joy or solace.

You are seeking shelter from some hurt or pain and you're trying to avoid confrontation. You're fearful and sometimes you're insecure. The difficulties of life have seemingly become too much to bear. You're overwhelmed and looking for a place to retreat away from it all. You would love a place safely tucked away from the emotional wounds and scars where they don't seem so prevalent. A place where your every thought doesn't go to that thing, that issue, that person or that memory.

Somebody reading this has said - God I just want to get away from it all. Although you've said that to God, you are running everywhere but to Him.

Some of you are hiding behind pulpits and titles. You can be the man or woman of God that pours into everyone while you mask your own needs. You speak life to everyone else while you need someone to speak life to you. You're dying while you're empowering others to live.

Some of you are hiding behind careers. You're the boss lady and boss man. You've got answers for all their problems yet you can't seem to get an answer for your own ailment, your own issue, your own thorn and trouble.

Some of you are hiding behind your gifts and talents. You are using that as your mini escape. It's the place where everyone sees the glory of your gifting but the half of the story is never really told.

Some of you are hiding in your secret addictions that you dare not let anyone know about. You're drinking, smoking, having sex, cussing and indulging in late nights. You're so worried about what man is going to say but forgetting that God sees it all.

Some of you are hiding behind the mantle of service. You are hiding in other people- throwing yourself into helping and taking care of everybody else, being everything to everybody but you're no good for yourself.

Some of you are hiding within yourself thinking that if you shut everybody out, nobody can hurt you but beloved you're hurting yourself. That's one of the worst things you can do to yourself. When you try to hide within yourself, you have to contend with everything going on within you. You have to contend with the thoughts in your mind that are constantly going here and there. You have no clear thought pattern and there is always something turning. You also have to contend with your heart and the condition it's in from this person and that person, this relationship and that relationship, this burden and that burden and your emotions that are completely out of control. You have to contend with what you see carnally versus what you heard in the Spirit.

You're trying to hide within yourself and pull on something within your spirit but your spirit is warring against your flesh and your flesh is pulling out all the stops.

God said that you must come from behind all that and make HIM your hiding place.

Child of God, there is a benefit of making God your hiding place.

David said blessed is the man that takes refuge in Him.

He was not talking about mere material blessings but he was talking about something that works on the inside. There is something IN the blessing that David declared.

When we make God our hiding place, God begins to empower us. He activates His authority in us.

In that blessing is also redemption. We begin to recover from the things that happened and from the people that have hurt us.

In that blessing is also reward. God will begin to repay you for all the hell that you've been through. It was Jesus that said whatever is right, He will pay it.

In that blessing is also resurrection. God wants to raise you up out of those dead situations. He wants to call you out of your grave clothes and cause you to have life and life more abundantly.

In that blessing is also exaltation. You may look and feel like you're in the low place right now but in due season, God wants to elevate you to the place that He has called you to.

In that blessing is the Glory. It's the Glory that God still intends to get out of you.

Beloved, if you make God your hiding place, He'll be everything that you need.

He'll be your advocate and intercessor.

He'll be your burden bearer and comforter.

He'll be your heavy load sharer and deliverer.

He'll be your shield and buckler.

He'll be your covering and protection.

He'll be your healer and your peace.

He'll be your safe place and your strong tower.

He'll be your restorer and reviver.

He'll be your banner and the lifter of your head.

Whatever you need, hide yourself in Jesus and He will be it for you.

David said blessed is the man that taketh refuge in Him and He summed up the benefit of hiding in God in Psalm 91.

1 Whoever dwells in the shelter of the Most High
    will rest in the shadow of the Almighty.[a]
2 I will say of the LORD, "He is my refuge and my fortress,
    my God, in whom I trust."
3 Surely he will save you
    from the fowler's snare
    and from the deadly pestilence.
4 He will cover you with his feathers,
    and under his wings you will find refuge;
    his faithfulness will be your shield and rampart.
5 You will not fear the terror of night,
    nor the arrow that flies by day,
6 nor the pestilence that stalks in the darkness,
    nor the plague that destroys at midday.
7 A thousand may fall at your side,
    ten thousand at your right hand,
    but it will not come near you.
8 You will only observe with your eyes
    and see the punishment of the wicked.
9 If you say, "The LORD is my refuge,"
    and you make the Most High your dwelling,
10 no harm will overtake you,
    no disaster will come near your tent.
11 For he will command his angels concerning you
    to guard you in all your ways;
12 they will lift you up in their hands,

so that you will not strike your foot against a stone.
13 You will tread on the lion and the cobra;
   you will trample the great lion and the serpent.
14 "Because he[b] loves me," says the LORD, "I will rescue him;
   I will protect him, for he acknowledges my name.
15 He will call on me, and I will answer him;
   I will be with him in trouble,
   I will deliver him and honor him.
16 With long life I will satisfy him
   and show him my salvation."

Children of God - there is a benefit of taking refuge in God. I encourage you to make today the day that you make God your hiding place.

Prayer: *Lord, thank You for being my hiding place. Thank You for keeping and protecting me in dangers seen and unseen. Thank You for being the Person that I can run to when life is too hard to handle. Help me to run to You first when things go wrong or right. Help me to know how to hide in You and how to seek You for all things. Thank You for reminding me that You are my hiding place above all things. Lord, I want to experience the blessing that is IN taking refuge in You. In Jesus Name, Amen!*

DAY 26
SET ASIDE

1 Peter 2:9-10 NIV

[9] But you are a chosen people, a royal priesthood, a holy nation, God's special possession, that you may declare the praises of him who called you out of darkness into his wonderful light. [10] Once you were not a people, but now you are the people of God; once you had not received mercy, but now you have received mercy.

I want to encourage every person that feels like you are alone. The Lord said take courage, you are headed into a different place with Him. For that reason you must be pulled away from some people, places and things.

This is a time of consecration and sanctification. You've been chosen for a purpose. You're being set aside for the next assignment.

As lonely as you may feel sometimes, you are not alone. You have been set aside.

Beloved, you must remember that whatever you're facing, whatever place that you're in has nothing to do with you personally. It has everything to do with your purpose. Your purpose is to represent

Christ to others. So encourage yourself – it's not personal, it's purpose.

The reason why no one is answering your calls is not personal, it's about your purpose. God wants you to talk to Him more.

The reason it seems that you're not being invited to hang out or even if you are, you can't enjoy it is not personal, it's about your purpose. God wants you to spend more time with Him. You're not alone but you're not supposed to be surrounded by them.

God wants to tell you things that you might miss if you're in the crowd. There are other things that God wants to show you that you may miss because you're distracted by what's going on around you.

The Lord said have no fear. He has not left you. He has not forgotten you. He's been working on your behalf.

Everybody can't partake of what God is doing in you and they can't handle what He's about to do through you.

The Lord said that He pulled you out for your own good. The words 'you ain't seen nothing yet' are not just a cliché concerning you. The bible says that eye have not seen, ear have not heard, neither has it entered into the heart of man the things that God has prepared for them that love Him.

Simply said, beloved, it's a set up and you've been set aside.

It may feel like you've been singled out. It may look like you've been picked on or put out but it's just a set up.

Take joy in this the next time you feel like you're on the outside looking in. You're really not. You've been set aside for purpose.

Be encouraged knowing that He chose to sanctify you. He chose to make you holy. He chose to make you more like Him.

This is your growing *and* growing up time. After you've poured out so much, this is the time that God alone wants to pour into you. This is a time that God wants to reveal more of Him to you.

God said that you've prayed for it. You asked for less of you and more of Him. Your time alone is how you will experience more of Him - in the consecration and sanctification process.

This is the place and time that you're going to go in one way and come out totally new. Your demeanor is going to be different. Your dialect is going to be different. Your motives will be different. Even your movements will be different.

The Lord wants you to remember the story of Joseph. To every Joseph, every dreamer – you are not alone. It was just a setup. It was the Master's plan to get you to where He wanted you.

You had to experience the pits of your life. They represent the places where you felt like you were left for dead and nobody expected you to survive. Those places prove that even in the pit, God had His hand on you.

You had to experience the prisons of your life. They are the places that you felt locked up, let down and forgotten. Those prisons, although some were self-imposed, proved that God would deliver you.

Now beloved, be encouraged because your palace experience will come in due season. Your freedom will come. Your season of exaltation will come. Remember that Joseph went in as what some call a cocky teenager with a dream but he came out a careful, prudent, thoughtful, mature man with a vision.

I would also like to encourage those of you who may identify with Queen Esther. You may have been an orphan or felt like one. You were seemingly unwanted and may have felt like you didn't fit in. Even among your family, you felt out of place.

Take a moment to remember her time of consecration. She was being prepared for the king. She was given beauty treatments for a prescribed amount of time. Beloved, there is a set time for your sanctification and you must go through this process.

Esther most likely went in shy and timid. She was an unknown but she came out with influence and the ability to make an impact for her people.

God said that He's about to increase your influence and you will make certain impact in the Kingdom. You're about to be invited into places that you would not have seen without enduring the process. Your request are about to be granted. Your suggestions are about to be received.

From this day forward, there is influence in you to make impact.

God has not left you alone. You're simply set aside.

I'll leave you with the Message Bible version of 1 Peter 2:9-10: But you are the ones chosen by God, chosen for the high calling of priestly work, chosen to be a holy people, Gods instruments to do His work and speak out for Him, to tell others of the night and day differences He made for you – from nothing to something, from rejected to accepted.

Beloved, you may have been separated for a time period. It may have felt like isolation at times. You may have felt alone but God said not so- you have been set aside!

Prayer: *Lord, thank You for setting me aside for Your purpose even when I didn't know what was happening. Thank You, Lord, that everything I've experienced has not been in vain. Lord, help me in the times that I feel alone or isolated to remember that You want more of me and I can only have more of You if I spend time alone with You. Help me to view my alone time differently. Thank you, Lord, for choosing me to be set apart for Your purposes. Help me to live out Your purpose for my life. In Jesus Name, Amen!*

Day 27
Forgive Quickly

Matthew 6:12 NIV

And forgive us our debts, as we also have forgiven our debtors.

This scripture is very encouraging to me. The key word in the verse is *as*. It means that we should forgive at the same time, in the same manner that we need forgiveness. When we talk about forgiving quickly, I want to encourage you to consider how you would like to be forgiven. Do you always want your wrong doing to be held against you? Would you like to be consistently reminded of your wrong?

I believe most of you would answer no to those questions. Most of you believe that when you ask God to forgive you, He does it at that moment. He doesn't hold a committee meeting. He doesn't debate over it or give you a long list of reasons why He can't or shouldn't forgive you. He grants your request and He is faithful to do it.

Forgiving quickly should be more than a habit; it should be a life style.

It is good to forgive quickly because unforgiveness is a distraction. It keeps you focused on things and people who have no relevance to your now or your future. Unforgiveness keeps you in a place where you only see what's been done wrong. It causes you to nurse your hurt feelings and negative emotions. Anything that you nurse has the potential to grow whether it's positive or negative.

When you don't forgive quickly, you are essentially nursing unforgiveness. You are feeding the pain and it creates bondage. You become enslaved to something or someone that only has the power that you have given them.

I encourage you to tear down the walls of hindrance and obstacles that have slowly erected themselves in your life through unforgiveness. How to tear those walls down may be the challenge that you're facing but be encouraged, God knows.

For those things that have taken root, you must forgive by faith and have a made up mind. Make a confession of faith that you are living in complete forgiveness of others because you need complete forgiveness. You may have to continuously make the confession and make up your mind daily that your actions will mirror what you say.

Going forward, forgiving quickly will keep the seed of bitterness from becoming a root. We all know that seeds are much easier to get rid of than roots. Seeds that have just been planted can be easily picked up and cast aside before they take root and grow. So as quickly as you are offended, you should forgive.

Forgiving quickly takes the seed of offense and the seed of hurt, betrayal, rejection, pain and so forth and it casts it aside.

Forgiving quickly will ensure that what has hurt you will not have a hold on you. It cancels out the potential of you always living on the defense.

Beloved, the unforgiveness that you're nursing is not hurting the person who hurt you. It's hurting you. It's holding you back. It's a hindrance to you. The forgiveness is not even about them - it's for you.

Forgiveness is so that you can be healed and free. It will help to clear your heart and mind. It will also unlock some blessings for you.

Unforgiveness on the other hand yields all types of disorders in your lives. It is the cause of some sickness and illness that have crept into your bodies. They have taken root because of what you're holding on to. Many may think that there is no way that unforgiveness is causing you physical harm but unforgiveness is a disease all by itself. It's disease. It's not comfortable. It's unsettled.

I encourage you to choose forgiveness.

Forgiveness fosters freedom and some of you need to free yourselves. Whether you need to forgive someone else or forgive yourself, it's time to be free. Don't hold your freedom hostage with a grudge.

Stop holding things against yourself that God has forgiven you for. Ask yourself- who am I to condemn myself of something that God has freed me from?

The sin - you may have committed. The wrong doing, you did it. The harsh words, you said them. But beloved, God said that the verdict is not guilty. It's time to forgive yourself and find your freedom.

I urge you to forgive now and do it quickly.

Forgive so that you can love freely again.

Forgive so that you can trust wholeheartedly again.

Forgive quickly so that you don't miss out on the God-ordained things in your future because you're holding onto ungodly bitterness.

Beloved, forgiving quickly is for your benefit. This is God's call to you to forgive them, forgive you and be free.

Prayer: *Precious Father, help me to forgive and do so quickly. I ask You to show me any areas that I am walking in unforgiveness. Please forgive me for holding grudges. Lord, I want to tear down these things are holding me back. Forgive me for not living in the freedom that You have provided for me. Thank you for not allowing me to die with unforgiveness in my heart. I pray that every day I will be forgiving to others AS you continue to forgive me. In Jesus name, Amen!*

Day 28
So, you agree with God?

James 2:14-18 & 26 NIV

14 What good is it, my brothers, if a man claims to have faith but has no deeds? Can such faith save him? 15 Suppose a brother or sister is without clothes and daily food. 16 If one of you says to him, go, I wish you well; keep warm and well fed, but does nothing about his physical needs, what good is it? 17 In the same way, faith by itself, if it is not accompanied by action, is dead. 18 But someone will say, "You have faith; I have deeds." Show me your faith without deeds, and I will show you my faith by what I do.

26 As the body without the spirit is dead, so faith without works is dead.

Beloved, what good is agreement if there is no power in it? What good are your words if there are no actions behind them?

When you examine the definition of agreement, we find that its meaning is said to be a negotiated and typically legally binding arrangement between parties as to a course of action. If you were to use the biblical term, you would simply say it is a covenant. And if you examine the word covenant, you will find that it is also described as a contract, undertaking, commitment, guarantee, a pledge and a promise.

There are some important things that you must know about agreement. Agreement is more than just words, it includes your actions.

With most agreements, there is usually some form of written document and within that document are actions that must be performed for the parties involved to be considered in compliance with the agreement. The question I want to pose to you is – are your actions keeping you in compliance with the agreement?

What is your agreement? Your agreement, your contract, your covenant is the Word of God. And it is your actions that will prove whether or not you are in compliance.

Let's be clear, you can't agree with it if you don't know what's in it. It's a good time to examine yourself and ask the question- have you read what you keep saying that you agree with. I'm referring to the agreement that is written in God's Word for those that believe in Him.

Too many people are saying that they agree with God's Word concerning them but the truth of the matter is that people are agreeing with people. They have agreed with what they've heard people say to them or about them. Or they are agreeing with God's Word concerning them when it sounds good.

Everybody wants to agree that the gift of God is eternal life but nobody wants to agree that the wages of sin are death. The power in agreement is knowing what the whole agreement says. If you know the whole agreement, then you know how to die to you and live for Him.

It is of no benefit to you to have an agreement and not read the entire thing. And when it comes to the things of God - I don't know is not an acceptable excuse. There are too many bibles in too many versions for you not to know what the agreement is and how to honor it. Deuteronomy chapter twenty-eight is your biblical proof that there are blessings when you honor the agreement and there are curses when you don't.

If you were reading a worldly contract, it would be called being in default. It's when one party fails to fulfill their obligation. Being in agreement with God is a privilege but it also comes with responsibility. Some of you are in default of the agreement. You are living with the adverse actions caused by your behavior because you have failed to fulfill your obligations. You haven't kept up your end of the agreement. You are past due on some things that should have been done based on your covenant with God.

Some of you are missing some key elements of the agreement but you still want the power to be activated. It's no different from the moment when Jesus said in Matthew 15:8 – "These people honor me with their lips but their hearts are far from me."

Your lips are saying that you agree but your life is denying the power. Your actions have to line up with your words in order for there to be power in your agreement.

James 2:26 says that as the body without the spirit is dead, so faith without works is dead.

You can't talk in faith and walk in doubt. Your walk has to be your words in action. Without action your agreement is null and void.

Null- meaning useless, ineffective, devoid and destitute.

But an agreement with action is powerful and full of power. So I ask you to examine your agreement. Is it powerful or null and void?

Beloved, real agreement puts the devil on the run. The devil doesn't want you reading, remembering or quoting a few scriptures. It becomes an even bigger problem to him when you start living it, walking in it and doing it because he knows that the power of agreement has been activated for you.

When you do your part, the enemy knows that God is going to do His part. When you launch out, God is going to make the way for you. When you go into those places that God has called you to and start those businesses and ministries, you upset the plan of the enemy because He knows that God is going to protect and provide for you.

The enemy isn't rattled when you come together and talking about what you're going to do. The problem comes when everybody gets their assignment, leaves the boardroom or hangs up the conference line and actually goes and does what's been agreed to. That's when the power of what you said is activated.

You might be agreeing with your words but the power comes from your actions. If it looks like the devil is running rampant and every time you turn around something or someone is blocking you and your efforts - don't even worry about it. You have sent the devil and his imps into a crazed frenzy because you have activated the power of your agreement with God. You must know that the devil is not trying to block anything or anyone that isn't moving.

If the enemy is bothering you, it's because you're bothering him.

But don't you fret or worry, all you have to do is keep doing! Beloved, there is power in agreement but only if there are actions with your words. Make sure you're doing what you're saying, living what you're preaching, practicing what you're teaching and walking what you're talking. The power of agreement will work for you but you've got to work what you agreed to.

Since you say that you agree with God, God wants you to prove it. Let Him see your work. You say that you agree with God and that you want God to do what He said but beloved you've got to do your part.

The power will be activated in your agreement if your actions line up with your words. When you get to work, it will start working. Things will start happening. Things will start coming together.

Even when the enemy comes at you, because you're doing what you agreed to, the power will be activated so that you can still produce.

There is power in agreement but you have to activate it with your works. Speaking it gives it life but working it makes it live.

If you need proof that your work will work for you – remember Abraham. James tells us that because of what he did, specifically James said it was faith and actions working together, and Abraham's faith was made complete by what he did.

I encourage you today to put some action with your words and activate the power of your agreement with God. It will work if you work it. You can not only agree with God in word but it must come forth in your work.

Prayer: *Lord Jesus, help me to get to work. I declare that I will serve You with my works and not just with my words. Help me to walk in full agreement with Your word concerning me. Lord, forgive me for the times I may have served You with my lips but my actions didn't line up. Today, I vow to work the assignments You have given me. I thank You in advance for Your power that will come forth. Thank You, Lord, for access to Your power because of the covenant that You have made with me. Thank You Lord that I am a problem for the enemy instead of him being one for me. Thank You, Jesus, for this word of life for my life. Help me to live it every day in Jesus name, Amen.*

DAY 29
WHAT TO DO WHEN YOU DON'T KNOW WHAT TO DO

Ephesians 6:10-13 KJV

10 Finally, my brethren, be strong in the Lord, and the power of his might. 11 Put on the full armor of God, that ye may be able to stand against the wiles of the devil. 12 For we wrestle not against flesh and blood, but against principalities, against powers, against the rulers of the darkness of this world, against spiritual wickedness in high places.13 Wherefore take unto you the whole armour of God, that ye may be able to withstand in the evil day, and having done all, to stand.

The bible declares that God will raise up a nation that will obey Him. In the raising of the nation, there is also reformation.

Because you are being raised up in God's nation, many of you have found yourselves in a period of reformation. Being reformed is not easy when you have been doing things a certain way for an extended period of time. Reformation can even feel stressful for some people who don't deal with change well. And reformation can be hard for those who are responding to the call to change because the attack of the enemy happens more often. Friends begin to disappear, family members turn away and co-laborers even look at you strange when you begin to walk in change and walk in newness.

When it gets lonely and you feel alone during your reformation period and you want to know what to do when you don't know what to do – the word from the Lord is STAND!

The book of Ephesians was written by the Apostle Paul to the church of Ephesus and these words still apply to you today. It was a letter written to encourage and strengthen the people. This letter reminds you that as a believer in Christ, you have been showered with God's kindness, you were chosen for greatness, you have been marked with the Holy Spirit and you are filled with the Spirit's power. You have been freed from the curse of sin and its' bondage. Amazingly, when things begin to happen, these words seem to escape you. Somehow you forget that God said He will never leave you nor forsake you.

I like Apostle Paul because while he encourages the people, he is also real with the people. Paul reminds you of who you are and all that you've been given but he is clear that this Christian journey is no easy walk in the park. He doesn't sugar coat it or try to make things look like something that it isn't. Paul was real in his message about who you are, what's available to you through Christ yet you find that there are times that when you simply don't know what to do.

In chapter one, you will find Paul saying that in Christ, God has a plan for you. In chapter two he speaks of your new life in Christ and being a part of the household of God. In chapter three, Paul urges you to be rooted and grounded in love. In chapter four, he calls for you to keep the unity of the spirit in the bond of peace, put away the old life and put on the new life. In chapter five, Paul simply said – and walk in love.

All of that great wisdom and instruction yet sometimes you still just don't know what to do.

In chapter six you get even more instruction. The Lord said that instruction is necessary for your reformation. You have to know what's wrong and how to fix it. And you have to know what to do when you don't know what to do.

This chapter is when Paul begins give instruction for your reformation period. There is something for everyone at every stage of life.

For the children – obey your parents in the Lord. Honor them. It's a commandment with a promise. Honor thy mother and father that thy days will be long upon the earth.

For the parents – don't provoke your children. Nurture and teach them in the Lord. Watch how you talk to your children and how you treat them.

For the servants and masters which can be equated to pastors and congregation or employers and employees – be obedient to the masters as unto Christ. Serve like you are serving God and not man. The bible says you should obey those that have rule over you and are the watchmen of your souls. Wherever you work, whatever you do, do it as unto the Lord.

I realize that someone reading this is going to say that's all good with the "instructions" and that you've done all of that and then some. You are probably feeling like you've done your very best and it still seems like things aren't going your way. I want to minister to the person who feels like you've done what you've been told to do and everything you knew to do. God knows that you've prayed until there are no more words. He has seen you as you cried until there are no more tears. You were not alone while walked the floor until the carpet was worn out. He has seen you as you read the bible until the words blurred. Beloved, God was with you. He is aware that you've done all you know to do and now you don't know what to do. The Lord said - STAND!

Beloved, God is strong and He wants you to be strong. Stand in the power of His might. You can stand because the Lord will hold you up. It's in your weakness that God is strong in you.

Jeremiah 1:18 says that God has made you a fortified city, an iron pillar and a bronze wall. You were made to stand.

Paul's message to you is when you don't know what to do, put on the whole armor of God and use what God has given you. Then you'll be able to stand. You must remember that your fight is not flesh and blood, it's bigger than that. It's the principalities and powers so you must put on what God gave you and STAND!

You'll be able to stand against the enemy when he tempts you. The bible says resist the devil and he will flee. You'll have the power to resist.

You can take a lesson from many bible teachers from Genesis to Revelation.

The Hebrew boys took a STAND in the face of the fiery furnace and without doubt they knew that even if God didn't deliver them, He was still able.

Daniel took a STAND when he kneeled down despite the king's decree.

The woman with the issue of blood took a STAND when she pressed her way through the crowd to Jesus.

Paul and Silas took a STAND in the Roman jail at midnight when they sang hymns and prayed. The bible says that the doors were opened.

And our Lord Jesus took a STAND when he laid down His life. He took a STAND when He allowed them to beat Him. He took a STAND when He prayed, Father forgive them for they know not what to do. He took a STAND when He allowed them to mock Him. He took a STAND when He laid His head in the lock of His shoulders. And Jesus took a STAND for you when He died and when He rose.

So beloved, when all hell is breaking loose, STAND!

When there is trouble all around you, STAND!

Through your heartaches and headaches, STAND!

When bill collectors are calling, STAND!

When you feel deserted and rejected, STAND!

When you're backed into a corner, STAND!

When it feels like the walls are closing in on you, STAND!

When it looks like there is no help, remember that all your help comes from the Lord and STAND!

When you feel alone, remember what He said. He'll never leave you nor forsake you. And keep STANDING!

STAND with the belt of truth.

STAND with the breastplate of righteousness.

STAND with your feet fitted with the gospel of peace.

STAND with the shield of faith.

STAND with the helmet of salvation.

STAND with the sword of the spirit.

Beloved, THIS is what you do when you don't know what to do-STAND!

You, child of God, stand and keep standing. This is what you do. Don't bend and don't break. When you don't know what to do – don't give up and don't give out. This is what you do. Keep holding on and keep pushing and when you still don't know what to do, the Lord says STAND!

Prayer: *Lord, help me to stand! There are times when I feel like I've done all I can and I don't know what else to do but now I know to keep standing. Thank You, Lord, for reminding me that You have given me everything that I need to stand with and that if I stand, You will stand with me and for me. Thank You, Lord, for your instruction. Thank You for loving me enough to tell me how to handle the things I don't know how to handle. I'm going to stand on Your word, Lord and believe You to come through for me in all things. I'm going to stand even when I don't feel like I can because I believe that what You say is true. Thank You, Lord, for strength and power to stand in You. In Jesus name, Amen!*

Day 30
It is finished

John 19:30

When Jesus therefore had received the vinegar, he said It is finished: and he bowed his head and gave up the ghost.

The focus of this article are the words of Jesus - It is finished. Beloved, that is God's word for your life – it is finished! That is good news for the people of God.

In this text, the IT that Jesus referred to was indicating that the mission that Jesus came to earth to complete had been accomplished. Jesus came from heaven to earth to die a substitutionary death for a sinful people. When Jesus died on our behalf, our sin was atoned for and eternal life through Him became available to us.

But what else did Jesus mean? I submit to you that it means more than it's over or it's done. Beloved, as Christ gave up the ghost on the cross, He opened the door to eternal life and He gave us something *for* the life we are living right now.

So what is IT? Everything from Genesis to Revelation, it is finished. Everything concerning you is finished. Whatever has been spoken concerning you, beloved, God wants you to know that it is finished. Every promise that God has made to you – it is finished.

I know that some reader is saying- I have not seen it. Beloved, you must believe that you will see it. You must believe that God has already done it for you through Jesus. You must begin to declare over your life - it is finished.

Beloved, the work of your hands is already blessed. The outcome of your situations have already been planned. Jeremiah said in chapter twenty-nine and verse eleven "for I know the plans that I have for you," declares the Lord, "plans to prosper you and not to harm you, plans to give you a hope and a future." When Jesus said it is finished, he completed the plans that had been made for you. Glory to God!

Whatever promises the Lord has made to you, I dare you to decree – it is finished.

Whatever plans the Lord has given you in dreams and visions, make a declaration today that it is finished.

Jesus reminded us that everything that His Father had already set in motion from the beginning of time was finished.

When Jesus said it is finished, you became the head and not the tail. At that moment, you were above and not beneath.

Because the scripture was fulfilled and His mission was accomplished, you can now be saved, sanctified and filled with the Holy Ghost.

Because Jesus said it is finished, there is therefore now no condemnation to him that is in Christ Jesus. What the law couldn't do, Jesus did on Calvary.

The law made us realize our sin, but the blood redeemed us. The law was like a mirror to show us our faults but the blood has cleaned us up. The law gave us direction, instruction and some foundation but the blood gave us salvation. Jesus said it is finished.

Beloved, I really want to encourage you to know that it's already done. It is finished.

The situations that you are concerned about, Jesus said at Calvary- it is finished. When Jesus said it - that sealed it.

When Jesus spoke the word, the word became life for your life. It is finished.

Everything God ever intended for your life is finished.

Every promise that God made you is finished.

Every healing that you need is finished.

Every answer that you're seeking is finished.

For those of you who feel broke and broken, your healing is finished for you.

If you've been a drunk or drug addict, your deliverance is finished for you.

If you've been backslidden, your redemption and restoration is already finished for you.

If you've been a gossiper or a liar, your change is finished for you.

If you've been tied up, tangled up and twisted in sin, your freedom is finished for you.

Because of the untainted blood that was shed on Calvary's hill, IT is finished for you.

Beloved, cast your worries to the side, dismiss your doubts and kill your fears because Jesus said – It is finished. And IT covered everything.

It means that there is nothing concerning you that God hasn't already worked out. You may have to wait for it to manifest but IT is finished. You may have to cry sometimes but IT is finished. You may have had some ups and downs but your IT, is finished. Sometimes it may look bad before it looks better but I encourage you to believe the word that Jesus has already spoken. It is finished. It's complete. It's done. It's over and beloved it's coming!

Prayer: *Thank You Jesus, it is finished! I bless Your Name, Lord, because all things concerning me are finished. Thank You, Jesus, that every question that I have has an answer and every problem has a resolution. Thank You, Lord, that my healing is already finished. Thank You, Jesus, that my deliverance is already sealed. You are a great and mighty God who has done all things well in my life and I give you all the praise! Thank You, Lord, for taking everything concerning me to the cross and sealing it with Your Word and Your Blood. I decree on this day that whatever my IT is – It is finished in Jesus Name, Amen!*

FINAL WORDS
From My Heart to Yours

Beloved, it is my prayer that you have been empowered, encouraged and strengthened to continue to seek more of God. My prayer is that these Articles of Encouragement have ignited a hunger and thirst for more of God, His righteousness, His Word and all that He has planned for your life. Thank you for allowing me the opportunity to share with you again. I don't take it lightly and praise God for you. I pray that you have received God's Word concerning you and that this book will become a source of God's power in your life as you go forward!

~Prophetess LaTrice Williams

ABOUT THE AUTHOR

LaTrice Williams is God's servant, first and foremost. She is mother to many beautiful children, two of which she had biologically. She is the CEO and founder of *LaTrice Williams Ministries* and *The Living With More* Brand. She is the editor-in-chief of the *Living With More* national newsletter. In addition to *Articles of Encouragement*, she is also the author of *Hurt to Healing* and *Life's Experience*.

As an ordained minister of the Gospel, LaTrice enjoys sharing the Word of God through many avenues. She will literally preach and teach her shoes off as she endeavors to empower, encourage and strengthen others to pursue their passion, live in wholeness and receive the healing that is available for their lives.